Matth

CHILDREN'S CHILDREN

OBERON BOOKS
LONDON

WWW.OBERONBOOKS.COM

First published in 2012 by Oberon Books Ltd
521 Caledonian Road, London N7 9RH
Tel: +44 (0) 20 7607 3637 / Fax: +44 (0) 20 7607 3629
e-mail: info@oberonbooks.com
www.oberonbooks.com

A catalogue record for this book is available from the British Library.

PB ISBN: 978-1-84943-234-4
Digital ISBN: 978-1-84943-520-8

Cover image © Francesca Carta

Printed, bound and converted
by CPI Group (UK) Ltd, Croydon, CR0 4YY

Visit www.oberonbooks.com to read more about all our books
and to buy them. You will also find features, author interviews and
news of any author events, and you can sign up for e-newsletters
so that you're always first to hear about our new releases.

In memory of Rod Hall

I'd like to thank Roxanna Silbert and Tessa Walker
for encouraging me to write the play, and Dennis Kelly,
Michael Attenborough, Jenny Worton and Jeremy Herrin
for reading it and offering generous and insightful thoughts.

Characters

GORDON
50 years old. Northern.
Lives in Blackheath, London.

SALLY
Late 40s. Northern. Gordon's wife.

MICHAEL
50 years old. Northern.
Lives in Holland Park, London.

LOUISA
40 years old. Michael's wife.
Educated at a public school.

EFFIE
19 years old. Gordon and Sally's daughter.
Educated at a private school in London.

CASTRO
24 years old. Black Zambian mother.
White American Father.

The above descriptions are of the characters as
we meet them at the beginning of the play.

The action takes place over four years.

Unless it is a question or an exclamation there
is no punctuation at the end of lines: Generally,
this indicates that the following line comes in
pretty sharply.

A / in a line of dialogue suggests the point when
the following line begins and overlaps.

A ... at the end of a line suggests the speaker has
run out of steam.

ALMEIDA

THEATRE

Children's Children was first perfomed at the Almeida Theatre, London on the 17 May 2012 with the following cast:

Emily Berrington – EFFIE

Beth Cordingly – LOUISA

Darrell D'Silva – MICHAEL

Trevor Fox – GORDON

John MacMillan – CASTRO

Sally Rogers – SALLY

Director, Jeremy Herrin

Design, Robert Innes Hopkins

Lighting, Neil Austin

Sound, Ian Dickinson

Composer, Paul Englishby

Casting, Julia Horan

Fight Director, Bret Yount

Assistant Director, Daniel Raggett

ONE

LOUISA Gordon and Sally were due for one of their
visits. We hadn't – I don't know – it was maybe
two years since we'd last had them over. It
had become less – regular – from having been
almost a monthly thing – that's a big change –
and to tell you the truth that was ok with me – I
mean they are – were – nice enough – I liked
Sally very much and Gordon could be really
good fun good company – but really they were
Michael's friends. And they had been a happy
foursome during Michael's first marriage and
Michael and Clare are Godparents to Effie –
Gordon and Sally's daughter and – I dunno
– I just – felt like – it was – it was the most
crystallized relationship left over from another
time for Michael and they had – you know I
never knew when they'd hark back to some
idyllic fucking time with Clare and Michael
'Michael and Clare' – and you know they're all
from the same – they're all from the North and –
but Michael and Gordon actually met at Drama
School – and they – they all just share – a history
an extremely affectionate history – Michael
had watched them become parents – that was
something else – another subject I was always
waiting for them to get on to – Michael not
having any kids – not with me – not with Clare
– but erm…yes they had this history – they'd
been to each other's parent's funerals – they met
up for every special occasion – and that means
so much – *so much* – it's real family that – I think
– yeah choosing to share – much more than the
fucking idiots we have thrust upon us by birth
– the choices we make to share these times with
these people – *our lives* – and I'd like friends
like that. I think that's maybe one of the reasons
I found having them over so…anyway – for
whatever reason we saw less and less of them.

Michael was so busy and they – they were less so – Michael was essentially – around this time – Mr Saturday Night – Mr Television – he'd moved out of acting – pretty much – and he'd been presenting since before I'd met him and he was incredibly popular incredibly successful and – it was a very good time for us – in that respect – and things just weren't happening around that time for Gordon and Sally. They were actors and it really wasn't – a good time at all. And they were coming over for a sort of pre-Christmas – thing.

Winter. MICHAEL and LOUISA's home. MICHAEL leads GORDON and SALLY in.

MICHAEL	Come in come in
GORDON	Freezing out there
MICHAEL	Hiya, Gorgeous
SALLY	Hello, Michael
MICHAEL	Ooooh give us a kiss you

MICHAEL gives SALLY a big squeeze and a big kiss.

GORDON	Something smells good
MICHAEL	Well – she's only just put it in I think you're / early aren't you?
SALLY	We've been talking about Louisa's food all week / looking forward to this
GORDON	Sorry, Mike we were just keen to get here. *(Calling out.)* SOMETHING SMELLS GOOD
MICHAEL	What yer like you?
SALLY	Flirting already
MICHAEL	It's only just gone in so you can't / smell anything

LOUISA enters from kitchen.

GORDON   Hurray!!

LOUISA   Hi!

SALLY   Here she is!

LOUISA   Hello, Lady

LOUISA and SALLY hug and kiss.

GORDON   Hey! Hey! Where's mine / where's mine?

MICHAEL   Come on quick he's getting jealous

LOUISA   Some things never change do they, Sally?

GORDON grabs LOUISA and gives her a big kiss.

MICHAEL   Hey get a bloody room you two

GORDON gives LOUISA lots of loud pecks on the cheeks

LOUISA   Get off you silly fool

SALLY   Look at them love's young dream

MICHAEL   Come on, Gord you won't want your dinner

GORDON   I will I bloody will I'm / telling you

LOUISA   Let me breathe, Gordon let / me breathe

SALLY   *(To GORDON.)* Embarassin'. How embarrasin'

MICHAEL   He's only muckin' about

GORDON   I'm not I'm not I'm in love

SALLY   Shut up yer loon

LOUISA   Yeah shut up

GORDON   I don't care who knows it

LOUISA   How are you, Sally?

SALLY   I'm very well, thank you, Lovely – great

GORDON   Ohh – to have a young wife

LOUISA   Gordon!

MICHAEL   Easy, Tiger

GORDON   What?

SALLY   Oh God – ignore him, Louisa he gets worse

GORDON   What? I'm hungry. This is just a little appetizer

SALLY   Ewwww – don't be so gross

LOUISA   Well, Guys – you're going to have to wait a
            while – Michael you told me 1 it's only just gone
            12 / I've only just put

MICHAEL   Yes that's what we said

SALLY   Sorry sorry, Louisa

LOUISA   God no! Don't / be sorry

MICHAEL   We can have a drink – it doesn't / matter

SALLY   Sorry

LOUISA   Of course not

MICHAEL   Do you wanna drink, Pal?

GORDON   Oh yes / please, yes please, Matey

LOUISA   How are you all, Sally?

SALLY   Oh you know. Building up to Christmas. Things
            are Ok. How's you?

LOUISA   We're terrific thanks / just really well

MICHAEL   Beer? Wine? Sherry?

GORDON   Sherry?

LOUISA   And how's – where's – Effie / and

MICHAEL   Yeah why not?

SALLY   They wanted to make their / own way

LOUISA   Sorry, Lovely, what's he

SALLY   Castro

GORDON   Not had a sherry / for

LOUISA   Castro Castro

MICHAEL	I'm into it. Castro! We're into Sherries – a nice Fino at the beginning of a meal
LOUISA	Castro!
MICHAEL	It's our new thing
LOUISA	How did I forget that?
GORDON	I know – fuckin' Castro!!
LOUISA	I don't know how I keep – I should just keep thinking the T-shirt the T-shirt
GORDON	Yeah go on I'll have a – a sherry then.
SALLY	What T-shirt?
LOUISA	He's on all the / T-shirts and the posters
MICHAEL	What T-shirt?
GORDON	That's not
MICHAEL	That's not Castro / that's the
SALLY	That's the other one
MICHAEL	Whodjamawatsit?!?
GORDON	Flippin' Guevara
SALLY	Che – Che – Che Guevara

Lots of laughter.

LOUISA	Oh of course it is course it is but you could see how / you could
SALLY	Yes / it's easily
GORDON	Yep that's the er…the trouble with your South American / revolutionaries
MICHAEL	Public school education!
LOUISA	Fuckoff, Michael!
MICHAEL	'E are – here's your sherry
GORDON	You can – ta mate – get / 'em easily confused
LOUISA	Where is he anyway?

SALLY   They needed / to call in and get

GORDON   Pissin' about

SALLY   Shuddup you! They needed to get something – something for his work a camera or a lense or something for editing or a boom or mic or sound or a light a special light I – it – I think it was a camera probably – I dunno – a – something for his work

MICHAEL   Painter and decorator is he?

GORDON   Butcher!

They all piss themselves.

SALLY   No he's a filmmaker –

MICHAEL   *(Sarcasm.)* Oh!

SALLY   Director

MICHAEL   *(Impressed.)* Wow!

LOUISA   That's great that's exciting – interesting – isn't it?

GORDON   Not really / he isn't

MICHAEL   What sort of

SALLY   Documentaries

GORDON   This is what he / wants to do he hasn't actually

MICHAEL   That's interesting

LOUISA   On what?

SALLY   Well he travels a lot

LOUISA   Brilliant – a film director

GORDON   He isn't

SALLY   He's very political

GORDON   Pseudo

SALLY   Obsessed with what Oil and Gas – big / business stuff

LOUISA	That's amazing – lucky old Effie
SALLY	She worships him
GORDON	Slow down Sally
MICHAEL	Filmmaker fantastic
GORDON	Can I – he travels – he's got a pretty nice camera and stuff that he got off his *Dad* and you can do all that – everything on a laptop now can't you and – he isn't a fuckin' filmmaker not by a long chalk – he wants to be he wants to be but, Sally – and he's got a few things to say about the big bad world as he sees it – everyone's a baddie – you can't drink a cup of coffee or switch the heating on without him lecturing you – he's filmed a bit of stuff about all that – but I don't see the point, Sally in trying to make them think he's successful when he most certainly is not that – he isn't – he talks a bloody good game you'll see that but that's all it is talk talk he…
MICHAEL	Alright, Mate – how's the sherry – poor kid
GORDON	It's not that / it's not
SALLY	Chill, Gordon / flippineck
LOUISA	Well I'm looking forward to meeting him
GORDON	Yes – yes – it's alright this, Matey – so you're into it?
MICHAEL	Lovin' it
GORDON	Funny little glass
MICHAEL	Copita
LOUISA	Don't get him started, Gordon
MICHAEL	Sherry, Sally? A tulip – the glass – the shape
SALLY	Yes please. I'll have one. I guess I'm driving
GORDON	Yep
SALLY	This is special then is it, Michael?

MICHAEL   Not really – I mean great sherries are cheap as chips in comparison to – say a bottle of fizz – this is a Fino – well actually it's a Manzanilla – which are put together in the same way as a Fino – Finos mature under a protective layer of yeast – unlike other sherries – so – there isn't contact with the air – they don't oxidise – and that keeps them lighter – fresher – lighter in alcohol. That goes for all Finos. But the *Manzanillas* are only produced in one seaside town

LOUISA   I'm going to – still got quite a bit to

SALLY   Can I help?

LOUISA   No it's fine – sit down – I hope he wont have bored you both to death / by the time I come back

LOUISA sets off for the kitchen.

GORDON   Go on, Mate – we're listening –

LOUISA   – So pretentious –

GORDON   – Don't be defeated

MICHAEL   Thanks, Pal

GORDON   Go on, Mate

MICHAEL   Yes

SALLY   Seaside

MICHAEL   Yes the Manzanilla is produced at the – (*Calling off.*) Fuckoff, Louisa – (*Back in the room.*) by the sea – in a town called – I need to look on the bottle...Sanlucar de Barrameda...and yes – in the town there's a cooler temperature – because of the sea winds I guess – there is more yeast on the protective cover over the sherry – and that yeast doesn't burn away as quickly in the heat of the summer so you get this

He sips.

SALLY   It's lovely

MICHAEL   More savoury ever so bitter gentle tang

GORDON   A little bit salty

MICHAEL   You goddit

SALLY   Like the seaside

MICHAEL   Yes – yes that's exactly it, Sal that's exactly it

SALLY   Beautiful

They sip.

GORDON   Do you remember those weekends in Dorset?

MICHAEL   Do I? I'm getting a place down there

SALLY   Really?

MICHAEL   Fingers crossed it's all about to go through

SALLY   Michael / that's wonderful

GORDON   Absolutely fantastic

MICHAEL   It's in the bay

SALLY   What bay – our bay?

MICHAEL   About five hundred yards from where you two
               got married!

SALLY   Oh, Michael

MICHAEL   We must never leave it this

               God

               It's fuckin' lovely to see you guys

SALLY gasps.

SALLY   Yes

Then bites her lip.

GORDON   Sally!

MICHAEL   Sally?

SALLY   Ok – Ok – its' nothing – I'm –

MICHAEL   You ok, Love?

SALLY   I'm just so tired, Michael

GORDON   Ring Effie

MICHAEL   Sit down, sweetheart

SALLY goes to her bag. She routes through it. The men watch her.

SALLY   I'll call her see where she is – see what she
            thinks she's

MICHAEL   She isn't late, Sal. We're an hour or so ahead of
            poor Louisa

SALLY   God I know I'm sorry I'm sorry, Michael

MICHAEL   No no I / didn't mean that

GORDON   Jesus, Sally!

MICHAEL   Just – finish that sherry – neck it – fuck the
            driving – have another

SALLY   Oh no I can't / it's not

MICHAEL   Yeah you can – I'll get my driver to take you
            guys home he's only twenty minutes away and
            he's got a mate who – or his son'll pop out with
            him and one of them'll drive your car back – I
            should have thought I'm / sorry

GORDON   God no no you don't wanna be messin' with all
            that!

The doorbell rings.

            Effie – that'll / be her

SALLY   That's them

GORDON   I'll go

MICHAEL   Shuttup don't be / daft. I'll go

GORDON   I need

MICHAEL   What?

A beat. SALLY looks from MICHAEL to GORDON.

I'll go. You fill her glass

He starts for the door.

Take your shoes off, Sal. Just flippin chill!

He's gone. SALLY looks up at GORDON. He stares down at her.

We hear MICHAEL and EFFIE and CASTRO at the door.

MICHAEL   Heyyyy – look who it is

EFFIE   Hi

MICHAEL   Hello, darling – come in come in – Hello

CASTRO   Hi

GORDON pours some water from a jug into a glass and hands it to SALLY.

GORDON   Just take something.

SALLY retrieves a bottle of pills from her bag and quickly takes one.

MICHAEL   Give me your coats and get through there and
           defrost yourselves. Go on

CASTRO   Thanks

MICHAEL   Go on

EFFIE and CASTRO appear.

GORDON   OK?

EFFIE   Yeah

GORDON   OK

EFFIE   Mum?

CASTRO   Hi

GORDON   It's alright

SALLY   Hello, Castro. I'm fine, Baby, I'm fine. Sit down
           both of you

MICHAEL comes back in.

MICHAEL	OKAAYY!
GORDON	We're all here – all your family!
MICHAEL	Great – it's great!

LOUISA comes back in.

LOUISA	Oh, hello, Effie
EFFIE	Hey
LOUISA	*(To CASTRO.)* Hello
CASTRO	Hello – nice to meet you

A beat.

LOUISA	I'm Louisa
CASTRO	Hi – Castro
LOUISA	I know. We've heard all about you
EFFIE	Mum!
LOUISA	A film – a documentary – director. That's very interesting
EFFIE	Christ

A beat.

CASTRO	I'm trying
MICHAEL	Drinks?
LOUISA	Well – over / lunch
GORDON	Yes please, Matey
LOUISA	I'm going to sit you next to me and you / can tell me all about it
SALLY	I'm OK thanks, Michael
EFFIE	I want to sit with Castro
MICHAEL	*(To SALLY.)* No you're not!
LOUISA	OK – well – we'll share him
GORDON	Effie

MICHAEL is refilling SALLY and GORDON's glasses with sherry.

LOUISA	We'll stick him in the middle
GORDON	Don't be so bloody / wet
EFFIE	You don't need to speak, Gordon!
MICHAEL	Drink, Castro?
CASTRO	Sure
LOUISA	And what are you up to Effie?
EFFIE	Writing
MICHAEL	Do you wanna beer?
LOUISA	Great. What?
CASTRO	Sure
EFFIE	For some magazines. They're quite, like, niche
LOUISA	Some kind of fashion…?
EFFIE	Kinda. Like, kinda not
LOUISA	Just that – you look very nice, Effie – very cool
EFFIE	What do you mean?
LOUISA	Well your hair – funky – God is that an embarrassing thing to say – funky – or cool – is that embarrassing?
EFFIE	I just had my roots darkened
LOUISA	Darkened? GORDON Darkened?
EFFIE	Can I have a drink, Michael?
GORDON	*Uncle* Michael! And who paid for that?
EFFIE	*Uncle* Michael. Not you! As if!
MICHAEL	What would you like?
EFFIE	*Auntie* Louisa
LOUISA	Don't be silly you don't have to call me Auntie
EFFIE	No. What shall we drink, Cas?

She pulls her jumper off over her head. She has a big baggy T-shirt on.

SALLY	It's because she used to call Clare Auntie
LOUISA	Yes
CASTRO	I'm just having a beer
LOUISA	Oh – I love that T-shirt!
MICHAEL	We're having sherry
EFFIE	Sherry?
SALLY	It's very nice, Effie
CASTRO	This is good beer
LOUISA	Is that an original – from the original Live Aid – wow – you weren't even born I guess – I danced on my friend's parent's dining room table to Bowie and Jagger – when I was little – in that T-shirt
EFFIE	If you're going to knock yourself out over some old T-shirt – you can have it if you like it that much
GORDON	Effie!
EFFIE	Tell him Mum – I *mean* it! I've just walked in why is everyone –

She stops suddenly and pulls her hair. It surprises MICHAEL and LOUISA.

SALLY	That T-shirt means something to some people, Effie, that's all Louisa's saying
EFFIE	Not to me – I'll have a beer too *please,* Uncle Michael
MICHAEL	Yeah – sure
SALLY	Really?
EFFIE	*Yes.* Cas and I are so alike – we're like – wake up – what time is it – no big deal – what we gonna wear – what day is it – what am I wearing – no

stress – what shall we drink? we'll just have a beer

MICHAEL   Well – it erm – must be nice to be so – spontaneous – relaxed – / spontaneous

SALLY   She's very impulsive, Michael

CASTRO   I've seen you on the TV, Man

MICHAEL   Yes – that's me I'm afraid

CASTRO   Good times

MICHAEL   Yeah – it's – it pays the mortgage – I enjoy it

CASTRO   Good times

MICHAEL   Yeah I suppose they are

GORDON   C'mon, Mate don't be modest

CASTRO   You're famous

SALLY   We're all very proud of Michael

CASTRO   What is that like?

MICHAEL   What is what like?

CASTRO   Fame

MICHAEL   Well – my stuff – the shows I'm doing at the moment – you're up for grabs – everybody watches it – I mean you say you've seen it

EFFIE   Yeah but we don't really *watch* it, Cas

MICHAEL   Oh   CAS   I do – I get a
                                        kick out of it,
                                        Man

EFFIE   Yeah but – everyone is gonna know you, Cas – but in a different way

CASTRO   Maybe

A beat.

             But what's it like?

A beat.

MICHAEL   Well

I don't get buses – or tubes – I have a driver –
on call – so – you know – I'm not big on crowds
anymore –

GORDON   Yep – must be a nightmare

MICHAEL   I was up in Manchester – which is where we
record the show – and I was walking along the
street – one of the main – shopping – and there
was a Big Issue seller – and I buy the Big Issue
you know and I – this guy said 'Big Issue' and I
said I already had it – and no thank you – and
he screamed at me 'come on your Michael
Stewart you can fucking afford it I seen you
on the telly you're on the telly you can fucking
afford it I see you every Saturday night on my
telly'

SALLY   Oh no

MICHAEL   And I scuttled off and got back to the studio
– to my dressing room and I was seething I
was like if you knew how much I – we – give
to various charities not just money but time
– Louisa dedicates a lot of time to – and I
buy your magazine even though I resent it
now because I used to think selling it was an
honourable alternative to begging but now
they do both if you say, 'I've got that one' or
'No thanks' then they ask you for some cash
anyway – 'Anything?' – but I buy it and what I
really thought was, 'If you are supposed to be
homeless and living on the streets then how the
fuck do you get to see me on *your* telly every
Saturday night' and I wanted to go back in time
and tell everyone who witnessed him screaming
at me what I do for charities – what we do
– Louisa does so much – and then I wanted
to smash his face in because homelessness

depresses me and I know he'll spend it on his
smack habit and then I wanted to be gracious
and patronising and imagined cleaning him
up and getting him seats to a recording of my
show – and make a big hoo ha of just how good
I am as a celebrity – be *seen* to be good and
change his life somehow but I also felt like never
venturing out onto the streets again or doing
anything for anyone and thought 'I have to get
out of this show I'm too exposed I don't like it
I've exchanged my anonymity for cash and it's
not worth it' but I still do the show and I still
take the money...so...that's what fame is like

CASTRO   That's a brilliantly honest answer

MICHAEL   To me that's what it's like to me

GORDON   You've got to ignore that shit

SALLY   Yes – you're doing so well, Michael

MICHAEL   I do ignore it that's what I mean I ignore it I
              never think about it except in those moments –

LOUISA   That's not completely true – you're so self
              conscious about – going out / where you can go

MICHAEL   I mean I used to love it – Louisa when I met her
              she said when she was with me she – in public
              – she felt like she was standing in a bright light
              that people could really see us – see her – didn't
              you, Hon? And that she loved it

CASTRO   Really?

LOUISA   It was new – for me – like a drug – people
              could see me – wanted to take my photograph
              – wanted a / picture of us –

MICHAEL   And it's bullshit – you know who are we really?
              I mean – who am I? It's not like we *deserve* it

SALLY   We always believed you'd do well – I've always
              / been waiting for all that amazing talent to
              shine through

GORDON   You were like this about adverts when we were starting out

MICHAEL   Yeah – well that didn't last

LOUISA   What about adverts?

SALLY   For you to shine through

GORDON   He wouldn't do them – troubled his conscience – I did them

MICHAEL   Yes and I lived under your roof – you were out sucking Satan's cock and I was living under your roof paid for by adverts

GORDON   If you don't do those things – nobody thanks you for it, Mate – and someone else does it and ends up with a better life than you – simple as that

MICHAEL   Yep

GORDON   You either live in this world or you don't and we do

CASTRO   It's not quite as simple as that

GORDON   Isn't it?

MICHAEL   Of course it isn't – but – Castro – I wasn't prepared to get my hands dirty but I was living off the profits so to speak – well Gordon and Sally's profits – we – my ex and me – we lived in their spare room – for peanuts

SALLY   We got our money's worth the amount of time you two stayed in and babysat Effie so we could get out

GORDON   Those where the days, ey, Mate?

MICHAEL   You were incredibly generous, Mate

GORDON   What goes around comes around mate what goes around comes around

MICHAEL	Yeah – that's right. Baby sitting, Castro, for little Effie
CASTRO	I can understand why you wouldn't do adverts
MICHAEL	*(To EFFIE.)* Beautiful
CASTRO	I've got a friend who does community and environmental stuff for Shell – it's just PR by another name –
GORDON	I did adverts, Sunshine
MICHAEL	I couldn't get enough of you, Effie
CASTRO	OK

EFFIE smiles.

EFFIE	Really?
SALLY	Castro's working – researching about oil companies for his / next project
LOUISA	Yes yes / you said. I'm very interested in that
MICHAEL	Of course. You were our cute little – little ball of magic. Now look at you
GORDON	Work is work and work makes work
MICHAEL	Still beautiful
GORDON	You'll discover that
CAS	OK
EFFIE	*(Still smiling.)* Uncle Michael's my Godfather, Cas
MICHAEL	All grown up
CASTRO	Right
MICHAEL	Filled out in all the / right places
LOUISA	Michael, you / old perv

| MICHAEL | I bet you're out every weekend driving your Mum and Dad insane with worry about what drugs you're taking – what clubs you' re going to – hardly any clothes on – loads of fellas lined up | GORDON | I'll do anything that's thrown at me – children – they need to be fed Mate – you've gotta put it on the table |

LOUISA   Michael, look around!

MICHAEL   Sorry, Castro – dancing all night – you lucky bugger – is that what you're up to, eh? Effie?

EFFIE   I'm not into dancing with drugs

MICHAEL   No no I'm sure I was / joking, Love

EFFIE   Drugs are for the mind not for the body

SALLY   Eff – Sweet!

GORDON   Here / we go

MICHAEL   Well – yes – I guess that might / be right

EFFIE   I like marijuana and I've tried heroin three times

GORDON   Come on come on come on

EFFIE   What is wrong with you, Gordon?

LOUISA   You see, Michael you shouldn't wind people up

GORDON   Please, Effie – this is / too much

SALLY   What will people think / of you, Darling?

EFFIE   I only smoked it – but I don't now because Cas doesn't like it and things have changed and some of us might be on a spiritual path

GORDON	Yeah – great – spiritual – go on – I'd love to hear about it
EFFIE	I don't want to talk about it
GORDON	No of course you don't
EFFIE	Work work work that's, like, how mediocre your existence has been
GORDON	Is that right?
EFFIE	Money money money –
GORDON	Grab grab grab
EFFIE	Some of us want to ask ourselves grandiose questions
GORDON	Like what?
EFFIE	Adverts? Selling yourself
GORDON	Who do you think you are?
EFFIE	Just because you fed me doesn't mean I have to like where you got the food from
SALLY	Please, Effie
GORDON	Spoilt spoilt spoilt
MICHAEL	This is
LOUISA	Michael
MICHAEL	I started all this
LOUISA	Yes
MICHAEL	With my 'woe is me for being famous' shit – sorry guys come on – let's have a drink – and – how we doing, Louisa – we nearly there on the grub front?
LOUISA	No not really
MICHAEL	OK
SALLY	Please let me help
CASTRO	Grandiose?

EFFIE	Yes
CASTRO	I don't know what that means
LOUISA	The lamb needs basting – it's Michael's speciality
EFFIE	The big questions
GORDON	Lamb ey, Louisa? My favourite
EFFIE	That *we* ask
GORDON	You knew – I love a bit of lamb – my favourite – sorry about all this, Louisa
MICHAEL	Ey come on. Family! We're family!
GORDON	Yes
MICHAEL	It's a lovely bit of meat, Matey. Highgrove – Charles' gaff. Suffolk Mule the breed is
SALLY	The breed and the feed
MICHAEL	Exactly, Sal that's all you've got to go on – the breed and the feed – they're a cross – Suffolk and the Mule – it's clover and rye which makes – the feed
LOUISA	How do you know this stuff ?
MICHAEL	Which makes them fat – they can't burn it off
LOUISA	Who cares!
MICHAEL	Don't know why – but it's that fat that's important – that's what you're really doing when you baste get all that fat back into the meat – got it from Lidgates – by the tube – Holland Park – bloody hard to get hold of – shit – you're not vegetarian? Effie? Castro?
EFFIE	No
LOUISA	I checked – come / on

MICHAEL   You see – you see who keeps this show on the road – really good flavour – slightly nutty – lovely meat – won all sorts of medals

LOUISA exits into the kitchen.

GORDON   What for? Swimmin'?

MICHAEL   Shot put

GORDON   Cyclin'

MICHAEL   Archery

GORDON   Triple Jump

SALLY   Baaaahsketball

MICHAEL   Hurraaayyy!!!   GORDON   Very good!

They all piss themselves.

SALLY   I'm quite pleased with that.

MICHAEL   The winner is –

He holds up SALLY's hand.

Industry medals – you know – food standards – Golds here there and – Egon Ronay – everywhere – I've had it going for two days in a lovely marinade – rosemary, sage, marjoram, oil, white peppercorns, star anise – gotta have that – cloves and Madeira err…oil – said 'oil' – and honey – yep

SALLY   Oooh gorgeous

MICHAEL   Honey and Madeira!

He kisses SALLY on the forehead.

We're alright. We're alright

SALLY clamps her hand to her mouth and nods. Holding everything in.

GORDON   Course we are – course we are

LOUISA calls from the kitchen.

LOUISA   Michael!

MICHAEL   Right – here goes – where's me Sherry?

He quickly tops up his glass and goes off to the kitchen.

Stillness in the room.

Silence.

GORDON is shaking – he closes his eyes.

CASTRO   Guys this is all a bit weird

GORDON   Let me think

CASTRO   *(To EFFIE.)* Why are we here?

GORDON   *(Whispering.)* OK I don't want – nobody raise
            their voice – I don't want a peep out of any of
            you. Sally – keep it together. Remember what
            we've said – why we're here for God's sake. Effie
            – I asked you – and don't raise your voice – I
            mean it – I asked you to come and help us – this
            is as much about you as it is about anyone else –
            I just needed you to help me for one afternoon
            – just to stop all your bullshit – and you can't so
            you and him

EFFIE   Will you please just Fuck Off!

*GORDON dives across the room. Skilfully he grabs the back of EFFIE's
hair with one hand and forces the other hand hard over her mouth. He
bends her head right back so that her body hangs – uselessly.*

SALLY throws her face into the cushions of the couch. CASTRO starts –

GORDON   *(Whispering.)* Stay where you are, Sunshine – I
            mean it

CASTRO   What's going on, Man? This is

GORDON   *(Whispering)* You can fuckoff with your fucking
            dog's name – you've got us in this shit. What?
            What? Fucking Castro woof woof like a fucking
            dumb pit bull

CASTRO   Sorry?

GORDON	Don't, Kiddo – I mean it
SALLY	Please, Gordon!
GORDON	*(Whispering.)* Sally – I'm trying to sort something out for all of us – and this selfish little cow – is – listen – you two are going – you're going to get your coats – and you're gonna go – we are all going to smile and be very polite to Michael and Louisa and I'll explain to them what's going to happen
CASTRO	You're hurting her
SALLY	You're hurting her Gordon
GORDON	Now – I'm going to let you go and believe me you had better not make a sound not a sound not a – you get what I'm saying to you? Do you?

Struggling – EFFIE nods her head.

Slowly GORDON lifts her weight forward then removes his hands.

EFFIE just stares at him.

CASTRO slowly takes her hand.

GORDON turns to face the kitchen door.

They all just look at the kitchen door.

Waiting.

MICHAEL enters.

MICHAEL	Looking good looking good we're still a way off with the roast
GORDON	Michael I'm sorry Michael – look

A beat.

MICHAEL	What?

Nothing.

Jesus – what? What's wrong?

GORDON   Nothing – look the kids are going to go – and – I
need to speak to you, Matey

CASTRO   *(To EFFIE.)* Come on lets go

MICHAEL   What? Why? What's wrong?

CASTRO and EFFIE move towards the exit for the front door.

GORDON   We're sorry about all this it's very /
embarrassing –

SALLY   We're so sorry, Michael

LOUISA enters.

GORDON   Louisa look sorry love but the kids are going
and I really need to talk to Michael

LOUISA   OK

CASTRO re-appears.

CASTRO   Sorry – our coats.

MICHAEL   Yes yes – sorry – I'll

He follows CASTRO out.

LOUISA   Are you OK?

GORDON   I just need to speak to Michael.

LOUISA   Of course Gordon if that's what you / need to do

GORDON   I don't know – maybe you and Sal can go for a
walk or something

LOUISA   Oh we could just sit in the kitchen

GORDON   Please / sweetheart I'm sorry but – yes

SALLY   If we could just go for a walk – I think it would
be more comfortable / for the boys

GORDON   It's quite a biggy this

A beat.

LOUISA   OK – sure – I'll just sort things out in there

SALLY   Thank you so much, Clare – shit – Oh I'm so
                 sorry, Louisa

LOUISA   It doesn't matter really it doesn't

SALLY breaks.

SALLY   I'm so sorry – Louisa

CASTRO and MICHAEL re-appear.

CASTRO   Louisa – I just wanted to say – I don't know
                 what all this is about – and sorry for any erm –
                 thanks for having / us – inviting us

LOUISA   Well I'm sorry this is – that we didn't get the
                 chance to talk – I want to hear what you've got
                 to say about – about the heating and the

CASTRO   Heating?

LOUISA   Sorry, I'm thinking of central heating I'm – I
                 meant *energy*. About the Oil – I mean your
                 documentaries, Castro – sorry – I hope we get
                 the opportunity – sometime

CASTRO   Cool – me too

LOUISA   Great – great – and – I didn't – what we were
                 talking – the light – this showbiz thing – the
                 attention – photographers – it passed – it's not
                 for me I'd hate you to think – anyway – yes

CASTRO   See you around

LOUISA   Bye

CASTRO   You're cool – it's cool

LOUISA   Bye. Bye

MICHAEL   Tara, Son

SALLY   Bye, Cas

CASTRO leaves.

LOUISA   Yes – I'll just

She exits to the kitchen.

MICHAEL   Hey, Sal, come on, Honey. What can it be?
            You're all scaring me to death

SALLY   I'm sorry

GORDON   Sally

MICHAEL   We'll sort it out won't we?

GORDON   I hope so, Mate

MICHAEL   We will we will I'm sure we will. Come on, Sal

LOUISA re-appears.

LOUISA   OK – that's – I've just turned everything off –

MICHAEL   OK, Love

LOUISA   Should we – how long?

GORDON   Half an hour say

LOUISA   OK – well – see you then

SALLY   OK

LOUISA   I'll take you around the park, Sally

MICHAEL   Wrap up properly girls it's brass monkeys out
            there

LOUISA   OK

They leave.

The men look at each other.

MICHAEL   Drink?

GORDON   Yeah yeah thanks, Pal – but – I'm kinda done
            with Sherry / I think

MICHAEL   Yeah course – what? Scotch?

GORDON   Yeah – a whisky'd be great

MICHAEL   It's just Laphroaig – is / that OK?

GORDON   Just?! That's great – that's perfect – love it

MICHAEL pours two whiskies.

He hands one to GORDON.

They hear the front door open and close.

	So, Mate? How is everything really?
MICHAEL	With me? Good – brilliant – why?
GORDON	No no – just asking – I know you're great, Mate – you should be – you fucking deserve it
MICHAEL	I don't know about that, Mate – I mean what does / that mean?
GORDON	You keeping your dick in your pants?
MICHAEL	Yeah – it's tough, Matey – it's tough – some lovely girls – runners – assistants working on the show
GORDON	Mate – you fucked one marriage up
MICHAEL	Come on
GORDON	Just saying – I love you, Man – don't fuck this / one up
MICHAEL	It wasn't just that – Clare wasn't well
GORDON	She didn't trust you – it sent her round / the twist
MICHAEL	She was no angel – you know that better / than anyone
GORDON	I know but we were all kids then
MICHAEL	And she wasn't well – this is – you asked me – and – this is just – a nice bit of fanny to look at – they're Effie's age so it's never gonna be more than just – you know
GORDON	I need to ask you something, Michael

A beat.

MICHAEL	OK
GORDON	Things aren't great right now.

MICHAEL   What dya mean?

GORDON   Sorry, Mate just let me speak for a bit –sorry

MICHAEL   No – sorry, Mate – go on

GORDON   No sorry – it's just – I mean – there's the
            obvious – career – it's all dried up – for me and
            Sal – she gets the odd voice over – but – more
            than that – more than that.

            I feel out of focus – you're – we talked about this
            as kids – you know your own level – there were
            some parties – people were either too posh or
            too well connected or just too successful – it –
            they weren't comfortable parties to be at –

            Remember that rugby playing cunt – you know
            at Jasper's house?

MICHAEL   What a cunt!

GORDON   Shaved my eyebrow off

MICHAEL   I heard him when he came back in the kitchen,
            'Thanks for bringing the entertainment down
            from up North'

GORDON   I was filming the next day

MICHAEL   We should have smashed that place to bits

GORDON   But I didn't – I sneaked out – humiliated – you
            fall asleep at a party and some toff – surrounded
            by all his officer mates and rugger boys – shaves
            your eyebrow off – and I didn't fight I ran
            because I shouldn't have been there – I was out
            of place – and that's what I'm saying – I have no
            place

MICHAEL   Of course you do – I wish there was a way of
            tracking that cunt down

GORDON   So what? For what? So I can say – you shaved
            my eyebrow off when I was a young aspiring
            talent – you thought I was a piece of Northern
            shit on your shoe – but look at me now! What?

I can't call myself an actor – I can't call myself
anything – I spend more time digging gardens
over for people – pruning rose bushes for – for
pocket money

MICHAEL   It comes in waves, Gord – you did / alright

GORDON   Yes – but I – those parts'll never come back – I
was shining with youth – I got the house – yes –
but that's gone

MICHAEL   You downsized – got a nice little flat – that was
sensible – pulling some money out of your
capital

GORDON   And that's gone – that's all pissed away mate –
and where is the next wave gonna come from
– you know what – you know what I think – if
we'd gone – if we'd had a proper education
– if we'd done – could speak Latin – done
the classics – or PPE – got a science degree –
medicine – whatever – went to a good school
– Oxbridge – all that malarkey – do you think
we'd still be dicking around doing what we're
doing? When I meet these people who went to
Oxford Cambridge and they're competing with
us for the same nonsense – I look at them and I
just think, 'You stupid silly twat '

It's like her – alright – Effie – she hasn't
bothered with university but that was a bloody
good school – and she writes about shit – fashion
– and people's favourite restaurant tables – and
they want her to model – ey? And she's thinking
about it! The girl who looks down on adverts?
Same thing! And this journalism – it's just
blogging really – no-one gets paid – no one gets
paid to write anymore – it seems – how does it
all work – how is that all gonna pan out – she's
skint – and – and this is crunch time.

MICHAEL   Gordon can I help you? Is that what – you
wanna talk / about?

GORDON   I mean – what does it mean really to be a God
            Parent – but she is your Goddaughter and we
            chose you because – of – of trust, you know?
            And because we knew, we always knew that
            you'd be there. And you never get to see – you
            never get to see her and that is never – that was
            never a – a thing because – because you never
            even get to see us – you're busy – you are really
            busy and successful – I always thought it would
            be me – there I've said it

MICHAEL   I always thought it would be you

GORDON   Yes – but it's you – you're Mr Saturday Night
            – you're the man on the telly – the face of –
            well – everything – everything that people love
            – people love you, Man – they do – *no* they do
            – they *do* – and I always thought that might have
            been me but I'm here having to – and it is this
            so don't say it isn't – I'm here having to *beg*. To
            beg

MICHAEL   You are not – this / is not

GORDON   It is it is it is that's what it is – and that's OK
            because that is what it is and you know what?
            You know what – Sally always knew – that it'd
            be you not me

MICHAEL   No, Mate, come / on

GORDON   She did – she did she knew even then right
            at the beginning when we all met and there is
            that big soup of who – you know – you know I
            always had a soft spot for Clare but Sally thinks
            the world of you and she says she knew – during
            that dance around when you aren't quite sure
            who is going to couple off – she knew it would
            be you and not me and – and maybe she wished
            you'd chosen – well she says *now* she knew – she
            fucking says that now with the benefit of – but
            that makes me feel – fucking – you know you
            are Mr Saturday Night Mr Millions Mr *Millions*

– and my wife lets me know in no uncertain
terms how she feels about me and that if things
had played out differently it could have been –
you – it could have been her – you and – and
I'm…

Pause.

MICHAEL   Jesus mate / you can just ask me

GORDON   Desperate I'm desperate I'm on my fucking
             knees you know I'm crawling round in front
             of my wife in this dead – this deathly – I'm
             desperate – I'm crawling around in front of you
             on my knees Michael – please

MICHAEL   Mate, Matey, c'mon, Matey – just say it tell me
             what you need and we can – money is not a
             problem – not a problem – it's fucking money
             and you and Sally and erm and Eff – Effie –
             that's – you want to be able to help – this is
             when the money makes sense – when you can
             help – we love you – you know

GORDON   Don't say that –

MICHAEL   But it's true – it's true – you're our oldest friends
             – mine – and that means – and yes you know
             Effie is my – my Goddaughter – and that has to
             mean – I mean it does / you know

GORDON   I need money, Michael – I need quite a lot of

MICHAEL   Look I've guessed that much c'mon c'mon,
             Matey – money is not – we're ok we've got three
             bloody homes – things are good – things are
             very – we're lucky – no kids – it's just me and
             Louisa – so

A pause.

             Do you …?

A pause.

I mean how much do you need to get you out of the shit?

A pause.

GORDON   It's…

A pause.

Jesus

MICHAEL   Please, Mate please / just

GORDON   Fifty – fifty thousand – that's what I need to get…

MICHAEL   Fifty?

GORDON   I'm sorry I'm so sorry, / Mate

MICHAEL   Mate! Matey! Listen that is not – Fifty thousand we can deal with – easily look if that's all it takes – look please – see – now you can relax – relax, Mate – please

MICHAEL puts his hand on GORDON's shoulder.

Please, Gordon – that's fine – and look

GORDON   I feel like such a

MICHAEL   And I'm glad you've asked

GORDON   That's what it'll take / to get

MICHAEL   And you've got it – you've /got it

GORDON   But I need – I *need*

A beat.

MICHAEL   What?

GORDON   Michael – I'm sorry – you don't under – you don't have to – it's different for you – you're Mr Saturday Night Mr fucking Saturday – it's different and thank you thank you thank you thank you thank you, Michael, thank you I'm desperate so…so

MICHAEL   But we've just – that money is

GORDON   It's a lot

MICHAEL   It's nothing

GORDON   C'mon

MICHAEL   To me – nothing

GORDON   You say / that

MICHAEL   I – fifty thousand – it isn't small change but it isn't far – isn't far off – it really really really isn't a problem, Matey – Matey really –

GORDON   That fifty thousand gets – the official – the banks and the – I can stall them taking the house and the car – that fifty thousand stops us and Effie that stops us not having a home – catch up on the mortgage and – short term keep the fucking wolf from the

MICHAEL   What do you need?

A pause.

GORDON   I can't say it – I'm so embarrassed

MICHAEL   Fuckin' stop that

GORDON   Sorry

MICHAEL   One hundred thousand!

A pause.

It's yours

GORDON   You are the best friend in the world – and I know that sounds a lot – that is so much money

A pause.

But

MICHAEL   You need more than that?

GORDON   Probably – I haven't told – you everything – I will – I will I promise – and however much you lend me – I – look if you could give it me in cash – I feel like a gangster – If you could give it me in cash – I have some control over it – you know

MICHAEL   Are you bankrupt, Gordon?

GORDON   No – God no nothing like that – I'm desperate I'm on my knees – it's breaking point – crisis point – but not what you'd call – not bankrupt – I've managed to keep the – I'm not insolvent – officially – legally – but the banks – you know – in order for me to make this work I just need to have power with it – control over it – complete – if it goes in the bank then – then – and what I'm really talking about – is – I mentioned the gardening – I love it – I'm good at it – you know how creative I am you think I'm creative don't you?

MICHAEL   Of course

GORDON   And I work fucking hard don't I?

MICHAEL   Of course you do

GORDON   I want to turn all that – that passion and – industry – into a business. But I need capital and I need the gear – to step up – to compete – serious landscaping not just pissing around with the neighbour's roses – and I can do it, Michael I can do this and just to then have – some sort of self-respect and – Sally – for her to

MICHAEL   One hundred and seventy five thousand. And we can work it out – the cash – also – me as an investor in the business maybe – we can do all that – this is – I've actually been looking for some sort of investment – this is

GORDON   And there is the – the biggest thing of all – I haven't – told you – you're her Godfather – but – what does that really – you know – I haven't told you because I don't want to emotionally – I

can't let it I wouldn't do that to you – it can't feel
like blackmail or something

MICHAEL   Blackmail? What are you talking about I know
you wouldn't

GORDON   Effie's pregnant – she's fucking – gone and –
she's pregnant – she's stitched me up – I love
her I love that girl you've seen it she's my baby
– my beautiful girl – but she's a selfish fucking
idiot – you're her Godfather – I don't know what
to do here

MICHAEL   OK and – wow – on one level I want to say

GORDON   Don't congratulate me please

MICHAEL   No OK no

GORDON   And this Castro kid

MICHAEL   It's all decided is it?

GORDON   What?

MICHAEL   They're going to

GORDON   Oh yeah they're having it – it's a fucking fashion
accessory isn't it? They don't think – no eye –
mind on the consequences – something to blog
about – twitter – whatever – fill facebook with
fucking pictures of it – but who is going to – me
– me – I can't throw

MICHAEL   What's his situation?

GORDON   His dad's a curator or something Chicago I
think – used to work out in Zambia – curating
some museum or – I don't know – his mum was
a model – but there's no – don't get the idea that
he has any – he gets flash presents – his dad feels
guilty I guess – but there is no real – his mum
lives out on some farm in Zambia with her new
family and – he – Castro is practically an orphan
– fucked up family

MICHAEL   I need you to name it then

GORDON   What?

MICHAEL   The figure – if

GORDON   Oh Jesus – don't make me

MICHAEL   If one seven five isn't enough then I need

GORDON   I can't

MICHAEL   I want to help you – and Effie – I mean – she is my – like you I don't know what this means – but – she is my Goddaughter and I – I can help so

GORDON   Two hundred and fifty thousand

A pause.

With that – in cash – I can clear the debts – hold on to a home – set up a business – get my – my – me – some of me back – look my wife in the eye – look you and people like you in the eye – and provide – look after my beautiful daughter – and my grandchild – and I'll make this work, Mike – I'll pay it all back – I can be a – make a real fucking success of this – I know I can – you're giving me a second shot – and my life back – you know that don't you?

A pause.

MICHAEL   Two hundred and fifty thousand pounds

GORDON   Look mate – Michael – I know what this looks like – Act One best friend asks oldest friend for cash – Act Two – he disappears

MICHAEL   No no I know that isn't going / to

GORDON   Well thank you – thank you for the trust – or Act Two useless friend pisses it all up the wall and comes back and asks for more

MICHAEL   No and that can't – that – there / isn't

GORDON   That's not me I'm not fucking like that

He puts his head in his hands and sobs.

MICHAEL   No no I know I know

               Gordon

               I know

GORDON   Good.

               Thank you

               Because – you know I wont take it if

MICHAEL   You're having it. Two hundred and fifty
               thousand pounds in cash. It's a done deal. It's
               about friendship. It's about trust. It's about love
               for fuck's sake. You're having it.

               Yes?

               Yes?

GORDON   Yes!

TWO

SALLY   Dorset means so much to me.

When Gordon and I got married – my uncle had
driven down from Barnsley and lent us his open
top car – and the four of us – spent three weeks
zipping around the countryside. It was bliss.
We laughed so much on that holiday. Michael
and Clare just stuck around for the whole
honeymoon. The photographs are ridiculous –
nearly every one has got a stupid set up gag in
it – the lads with sausages hanging out of their
flies – Clare with a sausage hanging out of her
fly – we found a dead mouse – dead but perfect
– and bloody Gordon wouldn't let us throw it
away for almost a week – and he'd put it in the
most stupid places – he kept sneaking into their
room and leaving it on the pillow next to Clare's
face – she'd scream the cottage down – Gordon
and Michael would have it on their shoulders
– in the photos – or when they were in the pub
ordering pints – bloody idiots – but fun – fun – a
smashing – brilliant time. And – one thing – we
didn't really know how to pose for the camera.
Now – you take a picture of Effie and – Christ
– turns to the side – head slightly dipped – eyes
up – I mean – it's her job I suppose but – *all* the
kids now – photo savvy – I'm friends with some
of her friends on Facebook and the photos – so
many – of them and their kids them and their
friends – and they all know how to look at that
camera – but we just had our gobs wide open –
laughing – jumping in the air – and we look like
– we look like we're gonna live for bloody ever.

God we were close – the wedding night – coke
– in the bridal sweet – I passed out and slept on
the floor – in my wedding dress – they were all
starkers – in the bed – coked out of their minds –
I could never go as far as the other three.

Clare needed a lot of help for her head – she became so scared somehow – and too much booze and too much coke – she didn't trust anyone – me – Michael – herself her doctors – she lives in Spain now – but we never hear from her – I heard she had a little boy when she was almost forty so hopefully she's OK – the boy will be ten or something now – it's fifteen years since I've seen her – and she was the best friend I ever had.

So – when Michael said we could use his new place in Dorset – we jumped at the chance – from the upstairs window you can see the little church where we got married.

I decided to – to get lost there – I suppose. Gordon would get so – I don't know – what he'd – business – work – finances – he'd closed up – I couldn't get anything out of him – he'd fly into such a violent rage – that I just stopped – asking him. I took no responsibility. I just let my good sense be swallowed up by Dorset – by the sea.

And I guessed that we were at the house in Dorset more than Michael was aware – I'm pretty sure he didn't know we took the family – but that was what I wanted – Effie and Farai to be near me – Farai stopped me thinking about things – beautiful little brown-eyed thing – beautiful.

And Castro found he could work down there – peaceful – and if Effie was called away on a shoot then I could help with the baby – I mean – we were pretty much – let's be honest – *living* there – and if we got the call that Michael and Louisa were heading down at the weekend Gordon would order us to do a big clean and – we'd scarper – we were never – no not once – never there at the same time – which now I know is strange or – and deceitful – I don't know – but yes – anyway – this day it all just took us by surprise – horrible – life changing – for Michael – horrible.

Summer. It's about eighteen months since the previous scene. At the back of a large seaside house. By the pool.

At one side a door into the house. At the other a gate to beyond.

CASTRO is sat – reading and writing. EFFIE is filming him with a digital camera. She wears a long shirt with long sleeves in a thin, cool material.

EFFIE   Here we have a portrait of the artist at work. Castro Blechman. What are you doing, Mr Blechman?

CASTRO   Reading

EFFIE   What are you reading?

CASTRO   Notes

EFFIE   On?

CASTRO   Harare

EFFIE   Zambia?

CASTRO   Zimbabwe – I drove across the border – last time I was there – you should / know that

EFFIE   What about it?

CASTRO   What about what?

EFFIE   Harare!

CASTRO   It's fucked

EFFIE   Come on Cas, why won't you like, play. I've got Farai down, for like, maybe like, an hour and I want to play. I want to know what you're doing you never talk to me about / your work anymore

CASTRO   Alright – I – you never– I took / Arthur

EFFIE   I never what?

CASTRO   It's good to have a real black guy around –
nothing – so – we drove through the night from
my Mum's – just me and Arthur and a small
camera – and – crossed – we crossed the border
at Chirundu – it's a beautiful drive - I told you
about the gig I went to didn't I?

EFFIE   I – sure – yeah I think so – tell the camera

CASTRO   They have this festival. African music and dance
– and – the – organisers – against the wishes
of the authorities – bus the people in from the
high density areas on the outskirts – and they
party – they find something anything to celebrate
– dancing – it was fantastic – so uplifting – and
dangerous – a big puppet of Mugabe came out
with blood on its hands and danced around to
'Never Can Say Goodbye' – just – amazing / and

EFFIE   How do they get away with that?

CASTRO   There are lots of dignitaries there – bankers
that Mugabe needs to keep on side yeah –
and a considerable international presence
– ambassadors – I was stood with the US
ambassador who just wanted to get home back
to the states with his dogs – hold on – that's
quite –

He makes a note.

I'd forgotten about him – he wouldn't talk about
anything in Zim just his stupid fucking dogs –
the Americans don't give a fuck about Africa
– yeah – so – safety in numbers – international
numbers, yeah? But the thing I'm working on is
– at the end the final song – they sang a version
of Imagine

EFFIE   Corny

CASTRO   Yes – maybe – but not there – not at that
moment – and they changed some of the lyrics
– and this was the – people – people held up

their phones instead of lighters – so the whole
field was full of these little square little green and
blue lights – it was great – we could film without
worrying – even though you knew the crowd
would be full of secret police – but we – only on
our mobile phones – we filmed on our phones
– and it was dark – the footage is unusable but
the – Arthur got some interesting sound – I'm
trying to construct supporting images – maybe
even animation – I don't know – but as well as
the phones a lot of people black and white had
their hands open – one arm held high and the
palm open yeah – it's the sign of the opposition
party – an open hand

He holds up his arm and opens his palm towards EFFIE to illustrate.

I loved it – I found it so powerful – the open
hand – about transparency – openness – honesty
– truth.

And

The next time we went back – just weeks before
the election – we managed

He stops.

EFFIE   Are you OK, Babe?

CASTRO   Yeah

We – we managed to get to some of the hospitals
in the outer parts of the city – and – look they
have nothing in the way of medicine – but the
real crimes – all the intimidation of potential
opposition supporters – murder for some – but
torture mostly yeah – takes place in the rural
areas where there are no hospitals – and medical
staff have gotta try and get them – secretly – into
the city hospitals – we found one doctor who
let us film – he held up the hands of some of his
patients – they take off their middle fingers –

they chop their fucking finger off yeah – so they can't make the open hand symbol

EFFIE   Jesus

CASTRO   Yeah

EFFIE   Jesus that's like fucking heartbreaking

CASTRO   Yeah

EFFIE   It's amazing what you do what you, like, put yourself through

CASTRO   I'm not going through it – I'm filming it

EFFIE   But you are and – I don't like hearing about that stuff

CASTRO   Well don't make me tell you then

EFFIE   I want to talk to you I want to – I get no attention

CASTRO   You get plenty of – you get more attention that anyone I've ever known

EFFIE   But not, like, not from you

She pulls the shirt up over her head and off. She is completely naked. They look at each other. He shakes his head and goes back to his book – EFFIE holds up her arm and makes the open palm gesture to the sun.

EFFIE   Openness – transparency – truth

CASTRO   We have footage of the hospital if you'd like to see it

Through the gate – GORDON and SALLY enter with bags of shopping. They take in the naked EFFIE.

SALLY   Oh my God!

GORDON   Bloodyhell, Effie – get some bloody clothes on!

SALLY laughs.

EFFIE   Why don't you, like, calm down

GORDON	It's not funny, Sally – come on – you're not a baby
EFFIE	I'm not allowed to get tan lines
GORDON	Well cover up sit in the shade
EFFIE	You're, like, so
GORDON	I know I know
SALLY	You'll burn baby go on
EFFIE	I never burn
CASTRO	Just get covered up
EFFIE	OK OK
GORDON	Thank you
EFFIE	OK OK

She sets off into the house.

Oh, the house phone's, like, been ringing, like, a lot

She's gone.

SALLY	Really?
CASTRO	Yeah a few times
GORDON	Did you answer it? You / didn't answer it?
SALLY	The house phone never rings
CASTRO	No – Effie said to leave it
GORDON	Yeah *don't* – best not to answer it
SALLY	Has your mobile rang?
GORDON	I didn't take it out with me. I'll go and check

He heads for the house taking his bags of shopping with him.

CASTRO goes back to his books.

| SALLY | OK? |
| CASTRO | Yeah |

Thanks

SALLY   You sure?

CASTRO   Yeah

SALLY   You need a break

CASTRO   It's pretty chilled here

SALLY   No I mean a breakthrough – a bit of luck

CASTRO   We're doin' OK

SALLY   Effie's doing very well, yes – that's not a
           criticism, Cas – I've just – when we were all
           starting out and Gordon was doing so well – well
           – it's never really happened for me – I did the
           odd theatre job and little bits on telly and – one
           big bit on a soap so people knew me for – oh
           about half a year

She laughs.

           But I wanted it – you know – to really be an
           actress more than any of our friends – Gordon
           wanted money – but I really liked the doing of
           it – I thought it could mean something – and
           when you are so committed – and I can see how
           committed you are, Love – then when people
           around you are finding it easier – and the way
           things have taken off for Effie – it can be tough
           is all I'm saying

CASTRO   I'm OK

SALLY   Good good – I'm sure you are

CASTRO   Look I can get some money – to finish off the
           Oil film but I'm not sure where it's from – the
           agency that is offering a grant – I suspect it's
           funders might not be too…clean

SALLY   What do you mean?

CASTRO   I think they might be energy companies

SALLY   But isn't that clever?

CASTRO	What?
SALLY	Taking their money and shafting them?
CASTRO	No
SALLY	Oh
CASTRO	It's not just them anyway – the film agency has all sorts of supporters who are looking to clean up their image by association with the arts or with charities, good causes, whatever – and I just think, yeah? I just think – with the kind of films I wanna make, yeah? – I've got to have integrity I've got to know who's funding these things
SALLY	But Effie's shoots, Love – they can't always be – she isn't always modelling ethical / products
CASTRO	That's Effie
SALLY	OK. And she supports you – and that gives you the time and opportunities to – doesn't it – and I'm not criticising honestly I'm not – to make the films
CASTRO	Effie's name isn't going to appear on the credits as a sponsor
SALLY	No but it's still
CASTRO	Sorry Sally but I really need to get on with this
SALLY	OK

A beat.

OK. I've got to get this shopping – got some lovely Sea Bream fillets – got to get this out of the sun

GORDON enters from the house.

GORDON	It's Michael
SALLY	What is?
GORDON	He must have been ringing the house – or Louisa must – I've got missed calls from both

of them and a message from Michael. Saying he's assumed we've heard – that it's an absolute nightmare and he's on his way down here – they've given him bail and he's gonna get out of London

SALLY   Bail / did you say bail?

GORDON   And the message is from getting on for two hours ago so – I bet he's not that far away

SALLY   What is it, Gordon?

GORDON   I don't bloody know do I?

CASTRO   And he said bail?

GORDON   Yeah on his – on his message yeah

SALLY   What do you thinks happened?

GORDON   I don't know I don't know do I?

CASTRO   We could look online

GORDON   Eh? Why?

CASTRO   Bail? He must have been arrested

GORDON   Yeah?

CASTRO   Someone like him it'll be on the – it'll be out, yeah?

GORDON   Fuck

SALLY   Do you think it'll've been on the news?

GORDON   I don't know, Sally do I fuck's sake

CASTRO   I'll get my laptop

GORDON   Thanks, Son

CASTRO heads to the door.

SALLY   What do you think it is, Gord?

GORDON   Are you fucking – give it a rest will you, Sal?

SALLY   I'm frightened – it's a shock

GORDON   We don't know what it is yet

SALLY   What could it be?

GORDON   And he's got a shock waiting for him – when he gets here – all five of us

SALLY   Well we'll have to go – I wonder why no one in the town / said anything

GORDON   We can't get all this lot packed up in – he'll be here before you know it

SALLY   I would have thought – well it wasn't on any of the front pages – of / the papers

GORDON   Well it might be something and nothing and the papers are miles behind everything these days – he's looking on / the Internet

SALLY   Someone would have said something to us

GORDON   They don't know we stay at Michael's

SALLY   Some of them do

GORDON   That's because of you showin off, / 'My friend, Michael Stewart'

SALLY   That fishmonger was a bit off I / thought. I don't show off

GORDON   No he wasn't what are you talking about?

CASTRO appears with laptop followed by EFFIE covered up in a plain cotton Kurta.

EFFIE   What do you think happened?

GORDON   Don't you start

SALLY   It's awful / Effie isn't it? Awful

CASTRO   I don't know if I can get a signal out here

EFFIE   Stay near the door

CASTRO crouches with the laptop on his knee. He taps a few keys.

CASTRO   OK – I'm on

SALLY   Oh, God I feel sick

CASTRO keeps tapping.

GORDON   There is something seriously wrong with you –
what could it be?

CASTRO   It's searching for the latest on…

He sees something.

Jesus

SALLY   What?

EFFIE   What?   GORDON   Tell us

CASTRO   'The TV presenter
Michael Stuart has
been released on
bail after he was
arrested last night
over allegations
regarding two
incidences of
sexual assault.   SALLY   No

The 55-year-old
was arrested in
London and taken   GORDON   What?
to a West London
police station.   SALLY   No – I don't

Mr Stewart, who
lives in Holland
Park, has risen to
fame in the last
decade with the
ITV show *What's
Mine Is Yours*. It is
understood that the
alleged incidents
are connected to
the programme   SALLY   But what is he
which is recorded   meant to
in Manchester.

have done? What?

Stewart, who is married for the second time and has no children, is currently filming the seventh series of *What's Mine Is Yours* where contestants can win the same cars and holidays and other lifestyle attributes of their favourite celebrity as well as a cash prize of £500,000' – blah blah

GORDON   Is there more about the – the – what he's meant to have – about the arrest?

'Last night a spokesman for the Metropolitan Police said 'A man has been arrested this evening for allegations of the sexual assault of two young women.'

SALLY   Oh god this is – this is awful

A spokeswoman for Fat Fred Media, which makes *What's Mine Is Yours* said 'Fat Fred Media is not making any comment

GORDON   Lies – it's gotta be

or statement on this issue this evening.'

Stewart was released on bail this morning, 13 hours after his arrest, he is due to answer bail on August 3rd.

A statement issued by his London-based law firm Hamilton Chard said: 'Mr Stewart emphatically denies the allegations made against him which have come as a complete shock and surprise. It should be noted that he has been released without charge. He has co-operated fully today with the police and will of course continue to do so should that be necessary.'

SALLY   Awful / poor Michael

GORDON   OK – so we know – he's coming down here and he's gonna be in a right state

A pause.

CASTRO taps a few more keys.

CASTRO   It's all over – it's everywhere.

EFFIE   Let me see.

He hands over the laptop.

SALLY   What are we going to do?

GORDON   We're gonna look after him – and Louisa

SALLY   Oh poor Louisa

GORDON   It's bullshit – it's gotta be bullshit and it'll blow over

EFFIE   Oh come on!

GORDON   What?

EFFIE   I've seen it

GORDON   What?

EFFIE   The way he's looked at me

SALLY   What do you mean?

EFFIE   His eyes, like, all over you

SALLY   What are you saying?

CASTRO   Effie – even this!

EFFIE   What?

CASTRO   Even something like this – you manage to make about you

GORDON   Don't listen to her – this is all bullshit – alright he likes the girlies – but he wouldn't force / himself on anyone

SALLY   Whadya mean – he likes the girlies?

EFFIE   I don't make things about me

GORDON   Well he got himself in the shit when he was with Clare enough times

CASTRO	You do
SALLY	They just drifted apart
GORDON	OK
EFFIE	Listen to what Dad is saying and, like, you know, see what he's like
GORDON	I'm not saying anything I'm not / suggesting
EFFIE	But you are you are
CASTRO	It doesn't prove anything
SALLY	They both had affairs
EFFIE	That he's creepy
SALLY	Shut up, Effie. Don't be so rude. Shut up
EFFIE	Don't talk to me like that
SALLY	Michael's a darling. He's a love. He's been nothing but good to us. He's your Godfather, Effie
EFFIE	Oh so what? As if that, like, means, you know, anything
GORDON	Just leave it will you
EFFIE	Look what it's saying he's done
SALLY	Yes *saying saying* / that doesn't mean it's true
GORDON	Just some silly little bitches trying to make a few bob
EFFIE	Michael is…

She starts to pull at her hair. Not too violently.

SALLY	What?
EFFIE	It walks like a duck
	It quacks like a duck
	It's, like, he's a fucking duck

A beat. Confusion.

GORDON   What the fuckinghell are you talking about?
             Ducks?

EFFIE   There's no, like, smoke, you know, without, like,
             fire

CASTRO   Please be quiet, Effie

EFFIE   No no why can't I say how I feel? It's, like

SALLY   Effie – you're upsetting us all Michael is a good
             man – he's / my friend and he's been good to us

CASTRO   Because you'll say anything to put yourself at the
             centre of the storm. Anything

EFFIE   *(To CASTRO.)* Why do you hate me?

She puts down the laptop and goes into the house.

SALLY   He doesn't hate you. Effie!

GORDON   Leave her

SALLY   Go after her, Castro

             Please, Love

CASTRO picks up the laptop and heads back toward the house.

EFFIE comes back through the door. She is pulling at her hair.

EFFIE   Why can't I say how I've been made to feel?

She pulls her hair. They look at her. She goes inside.

*CASTRO looks back at SALLY then picks up the laptop and follows EFFIE
indoors.*

SALLY   What do you think is going to happen to
             Michael?

No answer.

             What can we do?

No answer.

> I'm going to take – better get this shopping in –
> the fish – I should –should I get more – will they
> want to eat?

She picks up the shopping and heads for the door. She turns back.

> It's Michael. All this is happening to our friend

She goes in.

GORDON stands still.

Suddenly an involuntary snigger erupts from him.

Then slowly and carefully he clenches his fists in the air.

GORDON   YES!

He puts his hands by his sides.

SALLY appears at the door.

SALLY   I'm going to put the kettle on. Dyawanna tea?

MICHAEL and LOUISA appear at the gate.

GORDON   Yeah I will / thanks

SALLY   MICHAEL!

GORDON jumps.

GORDON   Jesus. Jesus fucking Christ. My heart – Jesus

*SALLY runs over to MICHAEL and LOUISA as they come through the gate
but then stops in front of them – not sure what to do.*

MICHAEL   You've heard

SALLY goes over to MICHAEL and holds him.

GORDON   Yes we've heard, Michael. What the fuck's
            going on?

SALLY   Lies

LOUISA   It's just disgusting isn't it?

SALLY goes over and tries to hug LOUISA.

GORDON   What's going on?

LOUISA   I'm OK, Sally, I don't want any fuss

GORDON   Michael – mate?

SALLY   Oh sorry / sorry

MICHAEL   I was arrested for Sexual Assault

GORDON   What does that – what

MICHAEL   Two girls – both on the crew – a runner – she was a runner

LOUISA   Twenty years old

MICHAEL   And err…Sharon…one of the make-up girls who has been on the show for four years or something – I mean – I know her

GORDON   But what's been said – what have / you been accused of

LOUISA   Tell them

MICHAEL   That I touched one in the lift – Sharon – that I rubbed her – crotch – while she was holding things and didn't have free hands – and that I told her other girls on the crew had let me do this – so she should let me – do it – and the runner – that she'd been called – that I'd had her sent – or called her – to my dressing room – and she came in to find me with my penis in my hand and that when she'd protested I'd forced her against the wall and pressed myself against her

GORDON   Jesus

SALLY   That's horrible

LOUISA   It's a nightmare

GORDON   So what happens now – next – what's – going on?

MICHAEL   Well I've been released on bail

GORDON   What does that mean though?

MICHAEL   Without charge

SALLY   Of course because they know they'll know

LOUISA   It isn't as simple as that, Sally

MICHAEL   My lawyer reckons / that it's while

LOUISA   He's been bailed while further enquiries take place

MICHAEL   That's it

SALLY   What further enquiries – what do you think that means?

MICHAEL   They might charge me at a later date

LOUISA   They'll be hoping for additional evidence to come to light

MICHAEL   *Hoping*? Why would you say that?

LOUISA   Oh come on, Michael, you're a fucking big fish I'm sure the police are as excited about this as everyone else will be

SALLY   I don't think so I don't think – that – people will want – Michael's so popular

LOUISA   Come on Sally don't be so naïve

SALLY   That's what / I think

LOUISA   Those police could dine out on this for the rest of their lives

GORDON   But new evidence? There won't be any

LOUISA   We don't know that. Where did this evidence come from? If two girls are prepared to go to these lengths – what's to say – who else is there?

SALLY   No one! Because we know it isn't true

LOUISA   They've gone all over the flat – they've taken some of his jeans and some shirts – whatever was in the washing basket – and they have the clothes the runner wore on the day

SALLY   So?

GORDON   Fucking – hell – they do all that? When is she
             saying / it all

LOUISA   Just a few days ago – the runner. The make-up
             girl – found her crying and heard her story and
             decided to come forward with something that
             happened a year ago or more

MICHAEL   'That *happened*'?

SALLY   But we know it isn't true.

             Don't we?

GORDON   Of course

SALLY   Michael? Louisa?

MICHAEL and LOUISA stare at each other.

LOUISA   Of course.

             They just need to figure out why these women
             would – concoct – this – it's sickening – I hate it

SALLY   And they will

LOUISA   But…he's a target

SALLY   Won't they?

LOUISA   *Fuckinghell, Michael…*what a mess!

SALLY   Oh, Louisa!

LOUISA   What?

SALLY   Nothing – I'm just so sorry

CASTRO steps out of the house.

CASTRO   Hi

Everyone jumps.

MICHAEL	What? Jesus / what are you	GORDON	Fuck!
SALLY	Oh my God, Castro	LOUISA	WHAT THE HELL?
MICHAEL	What's he doing here?	GORDON	Look look I can explain – I meant to call you to let you know – but – things just
SALLY	It's Castro, Effie's husband		
CASTRO	Sorry – I didn't mean to – I just wanted to say 'Hello' and that I'm sorry – about	LOUISA	Yes – yes of course
		MICHAEL	Who else is here?
		GORDON	Effie and the little girl
SALLY	Effie and Farai		

GORDON   We were gonna pack up and go – the lot of us – I didn't bother asking you about them coming down – sorry – I just didn't think – I didn't think – but – with all this – we were gonna go – but we thought – me and Sal – that we might be able to help – you know – look after you guys a bit – I dunno – I was flummoxed / mate

MICHAEL   OK OK I hear you fuckinghell.

A pause.

FUCKINGHELL!

A pause.

I'm going inside. Is there anywhere I can put my fucking stuff?

SALLY   Yes – we haven't – we never – we'd never use your room

MICHAEL   Good

MICHAEL picks up his bags and goes inside.

The others stand. For some time.

SALLY   I don't know what to…

LOUISA   No

SALLY   Maybe I'll make some tea – should I?

GORDON   Yes / do that

LOUISA   I'll have a tea – yes – thank you

SALLY   OK – I'll do that then – OK

SALLY exits she gets to the door and turns back.

          This is…it'll…you know?

She disappears into the house.

GORDON   Where's Effie?

CASTRO   She's lying down with Farai

GORDON   She's not asleep?

CASTRO   I – yeah maybe – I dunno – yeah

GORDON   Louisa?

LOUISA   What?

GORDON   How you doing?

No answer.

          I don't know about tea – I'm going to get a
proper drink – anyone – I – Michael'll need
something – I'm sure

Nothing.

          Just me then. I'll see if Mike…

He exits.

*LOUISA and CASTRO just stand there. We hear how peaceful this place
is – should be.*

CASTRO   This family I seem to have got myself
involved with – they are a nightmare. Every
time I see you – there's some sort of – well –

embarrassment yeah caused by this family I
seem to have got tied up with – we shouldn't be
here.

No answer.

I'm sorry to hear about – the arrest

LOUISA   Sally has a heart of gold – it's probably good for
Michael – she adores him – probably good –
that they're here

CASTRO   Yeah – maybe – but what about you?

LOUISA   Sorry?

No answer.

I don't want to see anyone – I don't want to see
– go down to the village – and – what will they
think – they'll think…

A pause.

I don't want to see Effie – I'm sorry – I'm sorry,
Castro – but

CASTRO   No

LOUISA   She makes me uncomfortable

CASTRO   I'll get her out of here – we'll go

LOUISA   I shouldn't say that to you – I'm sorry

CASTRO   She's an idiot – I'll get her / out of here as soon
as possible

LOUISA   Oh, Castro, you shouldn't talk about her like
that I'm sorry

CASTRO   You're really beautiful do you know that?

A beat.

LOUISA   You?

What?

Did?

CASTRO   Yeah?

LOUISA   This is…

CASTRO   Neither the time or place or – maybe? I dunno
            – I just thought you should know, yeah? You are
            very very beautiful

A long moment.

LOUISA   Michael is in – serious trouble

CASTRO   Is there any truth in it do you think?

Silence. A mobile phone starts to ring in the house.

LOUISA   Someone's phone

CASTRO   It isn't mine

LOUISA   It's not Michael's – not his – thing – thing

CASTRO   Ringtone

LOUISA   No – yes – I – I need to take these inside

Indicates her bags.

CASTRO   Can I help you?

LOUISA   No

A pause.

CASTRO   We'll go – when the baby is awake

LOUISA picks up her bags. She passes CASTRO and goes inside.

CASTRO wanders over to the table. He flicks at his notebook. He sits.

MICHAEL steps outside and lights a cigarette.

CASTRO glances at him and gives him a half smile.

CASTRO goes back to his notebook and begins to write.

MICHAEL   Ey? Ey? What you writin'?

CASTRO   Sorry?

MICHAEL   What the fuck are you writing about?

CASTRO	Nothing, Man, nothing
MICHAEL	Nothing?
CASTRO	Well – it's about – it – a trip to Africa
MICHAEL	I'd rather
CASTRO	Yeah – I mean – you can / look – you know
MICHAEL	I just don't want people scribbling around me right now – OK – for obvious fuckin'
CASTRO	Yeah – look – I'm outta here, Man – we shouldn't be here – you gotta whole heapa shit to deal with / and you don't
MICHAEL	What yer tryna say?
CASTRO	Nothing
MICHAEL	Guilty until proven – those fucking cunts – guilty – until proven otherwise, eh?

Nothing from CASTRO. A mobile rings – same as before.

	Whose phone is that?
CASTRO	Not mine – not Effie's – I don't know I'll find out

GORDON comes out with two glasses of scotch on the rocks.

GORDON	There you are, Matey. Here you go.

He hands a glass to MICHAEL.

	Scotch
MICHAEL	There's some left then?
GORDON	What?
MICHAEL	My Scotch! You haven't necked it all then – yet?
GORDON	I bring it – this is mine – I bring it

CASTRO has collected his notebooks and stuff and is heading for the door.

MICHAEL	*(To CASTRO.)* Anything said here – you understand – my business
CASTRO	*(To GORDON.)* I'm going to pack.

GORDON   Good idea. Good idea, Son

CASTRO goes into the house.

        I'm sorry mate. I fucked up.

MICHAEL moves away and sits down.

GORDON follows him.

        You can sort this can't you? Your lawyers? You can – it'll blow over won't it?

A long pause.

MICHAEL   So how's my investment going?

GORDON   Jesus – you don't wanna be talkin' about that

MICHAEL   You seem to be spending a lot of time down here

GORDON   Not really

MICHAEL   Really?

GORDON   No

MICHAEL   So

        How's business?

GORDON   You know

MICHAEL   No

GORDON   It's slow – summer – you know – people like to get out in the garden and do a lot of stuff for themselves

MICHAEL   What – landscaping?

GORDON   No – well – no – I didn't / mean

MICHAEL   'Cause I thought that was what you wanted to do – stop pruning roses and get into Grand Designs or something

GORDON   It's happenin' it's all happenin' just slow – you know – and that's – you know – one of the

reasons – down here – I'm making inroads and
it'd be good to get something going down here

MICHAEL   Fuckin'ell, Gordon

GORDON   I mean as well as – as well as what we've got in
Blackheath

MICHAEL   Money?

GORDON   What?

MICHAEL   You doin' alright?

GORDON   Like I said – it's slow – there wasn't a great
deal – after clearing up all my shit – left – left to
invest

MICHAEL   But I mean – Effie's doing so well – now she's
following in her old man's footsteps and sold her
soul to Ad Men. She must be minted –

GORDON   Well she's got the baby

MICHAEL   I know she's got the baby I thought I was giving
you money so you could help out with your
daughter – and your granddaughter

GORDON   But, Mike, I'm telling you

MICHAEL   There wasn't anything left once you'd cleaned
up all your shit!

A pause.

I am fucked

GORDON   No

MICHAEL   Yes

GORDON   You can sort this out – just bullshit lies

MICHAEL   I'm finished, Mate

GORDON   Your lawyer

MICHAEL   How to play it – that's all they're talking about –
how to play it depending on what comes to light

> – how to tell Louisa – and I tell you this – she
> won't stick around – she'll fuckin' clear me out

GORDON   I don't know what you mean – play it?

MICHAEL   If it pans out that it's just these two – then with
the runner – Natasha her name is – I have to
go for consensual – I can flat deny the grope
with Sharon – just deny everything – she has a
vendetta – something like that – a grudge

GORDON   Consensual?

MICHAEL   My lawyer said my cock only needed to have
touched Natasha's jeans and they could have my
fucking DNA

GORDON   What you saying?

MICHEAL   What do you think I'm fucking saying?

A beat.

> You see?

A beat.

> Howdya get outta this? I'm dead in the water
> mate.

A beat.

> And if this brings other stuff out of the
> woodwork – then – how many flat denials
> can you make? How many women might
> have a vendetta? Then you start getting into
> the territory of claiming to be a sex addict or
> something.

> And I'll go down – just too many – potential –
> if they can build up – decide to put together a
> pattern – of – of behaviour.

> There is nothing like this thing with Natasha –
> though – but all the other – voices – could make
> that stick.

I'm fucked.

Fucked.

I've worked all my life for this – and – you
know – they don't want us to have it – what does
everyone else do – with power – with money
– everyone everyone – can do what they want
– and along comes fucking muggins here – you
can't have it – not speaking like that – we'll fix
you up somehow – you're the court jester you're
not really part of the fucking club – you can fuck
off back down where you belong

GORDON   How old is she? The runner?

MICHAEL   Twenty – I think – something…

A pause.

Might be able to – settle – with some of 'em –
money. Out of court.

A pause.

Soon – I've got to sit Louisa – down – or my
lawyer has got to sit her down or both of us and
tell her – this is it. You do a deal – a bargain
with your own fucking wife – get her to play –
devotion – devoted

GORDON   You'd tell her the truth?

MICHAEL   I need to wait to see what else comes to light –
before I know which truth to tell her

A long pause.

GORDON   Another scotch?

MICHAEL   Yeah. You owe me two hundred and fifty
thousand pounds

GORDON   I know

MICHAEL   That's what I gave you – that's what you owe me

GORDON   I thought some of it

MICHAEL   What?

GORDON   Was a gift

MICHAEL   'I can't do it' – you said – 'if you don't believe
            me.' You asked me for two hundred and fifty
            thousand pounds and you asked me to believe
            you to trust you – to trust you to do what?

GORDON   That I could make a go of it

MICHAEL   That you could pay me back. Fuck you,
            Gordon. I need it. Trust me – these places – are
            fuckin' – to the hilt - mortgaged to the hilt –
            who's gonna give me a job? Ey – so – Act One
            he lends his best friend some money – Act Two
            he's gonna have to – have to get it back – 'cause
            he's fucked

GORDON   You're panicking.

MICHAEL   Fuck you, Gordon. I need it. Trust me. I'm
            fucked.

*SALLY comes out. She carries a tray with cups, a pot of tea and her
mobile phone.*

SALLY   I just made a pot. Do you want tea? And I didn't
            know if anyone wanted to eat

GORDON   We need to think about going

SALLY   Yes

A beat.

            Whatever everyone thinks is best. A phone
            kept ringing and I thought – I – well that it
            was someone else's and – but – it's mine – but
            it never rings. How do I listen to a message,
            Gordon?

She hands GORDON her mobile phone. He fiddles with it.

            I'll just pour for everyone shall I?

MICHAEL   Thank you. Thanks, Sally

SALLY   Oh, Michael. It's so unfair – unreal – I – you – if
             only they knew – the damage

She goes over to MICHAEL and touches his head.

GORDON   Here you go

SALLY takes the phone and listens to her phone

SALLY   Oh

             Oh

             Oh my God

GORDON   What?

SALLY   Oh

She ends the call.

GORDON   What?

SALLY   It's my agent

GORDON   Your agent?

SALLY   I know. He wants me to call him

GORDON   Why?

SALLY   I don't know. He said it was exciting

GORDON   But

SALLY   I know – I know – I didn't know he had my
             mobile – I never hear from them

MICHAEL   It might be the press

GORDON   What?

SALLY   Why?

MICHAEL   'A friend of Michael Stewart commented', 'A
             source close to Michael Stewart'– that sort of
             thing. Please, Sally

SALLY   God no I'd never – never – I'll call him – now –
             and if it's that – I'll just pour a tea for Louisa and

> take it in to her – do you think that'll be OK, Michael – will she mind?

MICHAEL   No. Yes, take it to her

SALLY   And I'll call – and see

SALLY heads towards the entrance to the house carrying a cup of tea in one hand and fiddling with her phone with the other. She stops at the door.

> Hello – oh – yes – hi – hello – it's Sally Turton here – yes – yes – Austin phoned – OK – yep that's fine.

A pause.

> Hi – hello, Austin – yes – good thanks – and you? Yes – oh – go on then

She listens.

> Oh
>
> Oh
>
> Oh
>
> Really? – Well – OK – how amazing – how strange – who would have thought – well I'm pleased someone – oh no – I haven't

Motions to GORDON.

> *(Mouthing.)* Pen Pen Pen

GORDON shakes his head and motions around him.

GORDON   *(Mouthing.)* Where? Where? Where?

SALLY   No sorry I haven't got one.

> Oh
>
> What and then I just listen to your message? OK – yep – I wont answer it – yes – bye – bye – bye, Austin – bye, Darling – bye!

SALLY ends the call.

> I've got an audition

GORDON   What is it?

SALLY   Well – it's a TV series – and – he – the director
             – watched me when he was a kid - as a – and –
             and he's a fan Austin says – I – look - I'm sure
             nothing will come of it

SALLY's phone starts ringing.

MICHAEL   That's great Sally

GORDON   When is it?

SALLY   Monday – I think – he's going to leave – I need
             to not answer this call and he's going to leave all
             the details on a – as a message – I'll take this up
             to Louisa and / then pack

GORDON   We need to pack – yeah

SALLY   Yep – OK – OK

SALLY goes into the house.

A pause.

GORDON   I'll get that whisky

He sets off towards the door.

MICHAEL   Just get one for yourself. I'm ok – out here. On
             my own

GORDON   Right. OK, Matey. Right

GORDON goes into the house.

MICHAEL just sits. He stares out. He doesn't move a muscle.

EFFIE comes out.

She looks at him. He senses her presence and turns to her.

MICHAEL   Oh, hi, Effie.

EFFIE looks at him.

             You alright?

EFFIE lifts her Kurta over her head and off.

What are you doing?

She stands naked.

Effie.

She holds her arm above her head with an open palm.

What are you doing what the fuck is this?

EFFIE   Truth – openness – and transparency

MICHAEL   What?

What?

LOUISA walks out holding her cup of tea. She sees EFFIE and freezes.

MICHAEL sees LOUISA and freezes. EFFIE turns and sees LOUISA.

EFFIE   Hi, Louisa. Swim?

She jumps into the pool.

MICHAEL and LOUISA stare at each other.

THREE

CASTRO   Well – I thought I'd met a rebel. The way Effie dressed, yeah? A kind of fuck off there are no rules attitude to clothes. Things were different with her – she was so sensitive so finely tuned to her idea of what was unjust. It was like she had a layer of skin missing.

Yeah.

You know?

I was kind of bewitched by her spasms when she felt things were unjust. Her resistance to her Dad, yeah, and his fucked up – aggressive – paternal control. Her desire to understand what I was doing. But her own drive to write to create to find new things and new people, you know? Her way of talking – affected – but innocent – she spoke in a way that I felt was like sketches for songs. There was a rhythm that could hide what she was saying – but she was always saying exactly what she thought. A brutal honesty.

I thought I'd met a rebel.

But I'd also met a princess.

And she ended up – well – is being good at wearing clothes and having your picture taken – is that creativity?

And does it matter?

The world revolves around her – or her and Farai – but that's the same thing. Her world – her baby – at the centre no matter what the costs.

She's a crazy maker – her behaviour – always affecting – other people –

Like

She was always crying. Always smoking.
Never eats. Always late. Left at inappropriate
moments and made a big fucking fuss about it.
Flirts instead of listens. Understands what is to
her advantage to understand – makes no effort
otherwise – only laughs when it's at someone
else's misfortune.

No that's not fair.

I don't know.

I find myself in the spectacularly depressing and
compromising situation…where the mother of
my child is not someone I particularly like.

But I mean Jesus – with that family – Jesus – and
I know you're not supposed to speak badly of
the – I know that – but – her family!

I've only seen my Dad about say…fifteen –
twenty times – I think that was probably hard
for my Mum, yeah? But she was a model – I
know I know I'm a hypocrite – but she's my
Mum and she's nice – and me and Mum
travelled – a lot – so – I never got the sense that
we needed my Dad – he gets me a nice present
when I do see him – he's got a cool apartment
in Chicago that I loved visiting – he gets me
tickets for things – he's put me in touch with a
few useful contacts – OK, I don't even know if
he can remember my daughter's name – but I
always thought 'this guy's cool – he seems to like
having me around – he talks to me – he listens
to me – he's a nice guy' – but Effie's family…

I don't get it.

So much noise – so much arguing – but they're
doing 'it' for each other – whatever 'it' is.
They're in 'it' together. But so what? If all you
do is hurt each other get in each other's way.
They were like violent boozy circus freaks,

yeah? All stuffed together in this little caravan. Her and her Dad – fighting and arguing and laughin' at each other's disfigurements. But sticking together and moving from town to town and pissing off all the locals wherever they go.

Things changed when Sally got that job. It's a big series and suddenly she had some money and that gave her a voice – and of course people knew who she was and that seemed to make Gordon shrink. Successful daughter – successful wife. I think it was too much for him – more bitterness – more stress – more alcohol – more rage – and that's what did for him I think, yeah? The rage killed him.

At the funeral – I'll be honest – I was excited because there was someone there I wanted to see. I hadn't seen Louisa for couple of years but I knew she'd be there. I hoped – and it was great – I mean to see her – not the funeral – but then of course we got more than we bargained for – no one expected him to turn up – but he – was – desperate – I suppose…yeah.

Winter. It's about two and a half years since the previous scene. SALLY's kitchen. It is modern and beautifully equipped.

SALLY enters with some trays – bits of food left on them.

LOUISA follows just behind – carrying some dirty plates.

They are both dressed very smartly – in black.

SALLY   Oh, Louisa, please – you don't need to – the catering – the girls they'll sort out all this stuff – they come back in the morning to clean it all up

LOUISA   It's OK it's only a few plates

SALLY   Thank God everyone's nearly gone – I'm exhausted

LOUISA   You must be – well – I'm going to go / soon

SALLY	No no, Louisa – not you – I – please stay – I mean – I thought you might even stay the night – Farai loved you – you were such a help with her today – thank you, Louisa
LOUISA	No no don't be silly / it was a pleasure
SALLY	No really thank you – she's a wonderful child don't you think?
LOUISA	Wonderful – beautiful
SALLY	Good-looking parents
LOUISA	Indeed

A pause.

	How are you doing?
SALLY	Oh – you know
LOUISA	No – I can't imagine to be honest
SALLY	The hardest thing – I shouldn't – perhaps – you
LOUISA	Go on
SALLY	Things take you by surprise – I wanted to – I don't know what I wanted to do – but I didn't expect to get wound up – by – this is not very charitable
LOUISA	It's OK you know – who wound you up?
SALLY	Well – the hardest thing was – seeing Clare – and I know that must have been even harder for you
LOUISA	No no no – not at all
SALLY	Really?
LOUISA	I mean I don't know her do I
SALLY	Well – no – / but
LOUISA	And I don't really think too much about Michael – now

SALLY   Really?

LOUISA   If I can help it

SALLY   I'm sorry

LOUISA   Sally please don't be sorry for me – think about
            yourself today. Please

SALLY   I don't know how to feel

LOUISA   No

SALLY   But I didn't expect that something was gonna get
            hold of me and piss me off

LOUISA   Clare did?

SALLY   Her…being here

LOUISA   I thought it was amazing actually – I mean – I
            thought it would have been – for you – I mean

SALLY   Yes

LOUISA   Why was it hard, Lovely?

SALLY   Because she'd *changed.* And – she looks like she
            lives in a different world – I mean like she's
            escaped from this one – and yes – yes I'm lucky
            – with the series – so maybe I've got what I've
            always wanted – I'm an actress on the telly –
            people like me people *rate* me – and I've got
            Effie and Farai but – they're the – the rewards
            for *this* life in *this* world – and Clare – in her
            skirts and her sandals and her long hair and her
            relaxed manner and her teeth are a bit brown
            but you can tell she doesn't care and she kind
            of smells of the hills and of little white villages
            and the sea breeze all salt and air – and I bet she
            paints and makes her own fucking jewellery –
            and I thought – she owed me some of that – she
            got away – caused all sorts of trouble then got
            away and left us to – to live this life – that – yes
            that she owes me and that it isn't quite fair and
            that doesn't make any kind of sense does it?

LOUISA   Well I don't know what you mean by causing
                trouble…

SALLY looks at LOUISA but doesn't say anything.

                I don't know – but it's easy – and natural at
                times like this to – take stock I suppose and –
                compare…

A pause. SALLY just looks.

                But – I – I didn't mean to unlock – I meant –
                when I asked – obviously – how are you doing –
                I was talking about Gordon – obviously – sorry

SALLY   Gordon?

LOUISA   Yes, Darling

SALLY   Oh I don't know. I guess it's going to take a long
                time to get to a place where I'll miss him calling
                me a cunt

A beat.

LOUISA   Jesus

SALLY   Sorry sorry

LOUISA   Jesus, Sally – Jesus really? That's awful

EFFIE comes into the kitchen.

EFFIE   Mum, please get rid of that Daniel and his
                horrific Australian woman. They're, like, such
                hangers on. As long as there is booze they'll be,
                like, stuck to the furniture. There's just them
                and Gordon's Uncle who keeps nodding off and
                dribbling on his shirt – if we can get them out of
                here then we can, like, you know, relax. Oh and
                Louisa

SALLY   I'm trying to convince Louisa to stay

EFFIE   Oh, really? OK

SALLY   Yes – of course – well Louisa doesn't have a
         place in London – since – anymore – and – you
         know – you will stay won't you?

LOUISA   I think I'll have a cup of tea or something and
         then just see how I feel it that's OK?

SALLY   Of course it is – as long as you're hearing that
         I want you to stay. Effie, beautiful, make Louisa
         a cup of tea please, will you? While I try and
         move people out

EFFIE   Good luck

SALLY leaves the kitchen.

EFFIE plays with her hair.

         Oh, your tea

LOUISA   If you point me in the right direction I can make
         it – easily

EFFIE   *(Pointing.)* Kettle. Teas

LOUISA   Thank you.

She begins making tea.

         Do you want anything, Effie?

EFFIE   If there's Nettle I'll have a Nettle Tea

LOUISA   Nettle?

She searches.

         I don't think so

EFFIE   Is that your bag?

LOUISA   No – isn't it your Mum's?

EFFIE   Must be new – for today – can you see if there's
         a mirror in there?

A beat.

LOUISA picks up the bag and hands it to EFFIE.

EFFIE looks into the bag. She takes out a mirror – pulls at her hair – rolls some black crap out of her eyes etc.

Don't you think Farai looks like me?

LOUISA   Err…yeah – yeah

EFFIE   I mean obviously she's got Cas' colouring and
            her little fro, but – the structure of her face –
            what, like, she really looks like – is me

LOUISA   Yeah – I can see that

EFFIE   It's important

LOUISA   Right – OK

EFFIE   Business

A beat.

            My business

A beat.

            Well if you're not going to ask

LOUISA   What do you mean, Effie? Sorry, I don't know
            what you mean

The kettle boils through the following.

EFFIE   I'm launching this range – the first stuff, like,
            that I have a hand in, like, designing. It's for
            me and Farai. It's for mothers and daughters.
            You know – so – it's nice isn't it, you know, like,
            when you dress your little girl up in clothes like
            your own – but these will be, like, exactly the
            same. So I have a sand coloured suede smock
            and Farai has an identical one – I wear some
            high wasted white flares – so does Farai – grey
            skinny jeans – like, whatever. But also we'll
            market a lot of the outfits as being event specific
            – so stuff you might wear at a wedding – like,
            we have these gold trouser suits yeah – or, like,
            a garden party – we've got these white maxi
            dresses covered with a summer fruit print and

it's about me and Farai our story is, like, in there
– my travelling my creativity – my style my
body even – yes – who I am – and Farai – her
heritage – Africa – we are using lots of colours
influenced by that continent and it's about
conservation, or awareness of conservation more
specifically. My marketing guys have this saying
– what people really want is just *A Conversation
About Conservation.* That's enough to make them
think they are *doing something.* So yes – in that
way – it's about all the ethical stuff which Farai
will inherit from her father – which people want
now – they want to know about it – it makes
them spend more. And ethically it's like – it's
about, like, about not wanting everything made
in, like, fucking Mumbai in a sweatshop – but –
Jesus – when you do the numbers – I mean we
really are against that – but the alternatives – it's
just impossible – so you find out that there are
sweatshops and then there are – other, like – not
so – you know, like – shops with standards –
how the machinists are treated – it's still India
– but – I mean the materials – are all ethical –
organic – the best natural materials sourced in
a very very…err…sympathetic way – but – our
man in Mumbai – because you do have to end
up, like, going to India to get this stuff made
– he guarantees that the production is – you
know – like, non exploitative – so – you have
to take his word. I don't have time – it would
be inconvenient for me to, like, go to India – to
see for myself – there is too much going on here
for me. Mum is talking to her producers about
me getting a guest spot on her show and – that's
something I want to put a lot of my, like, energy
into – being an actress. So I – have to prioritise
my energies – but the main thing is – that the
people who buy my clothes – what is touching
their skin will be nice – good natural materials

– nice – on their skin. For mothers and their children

Throughout this LOUISA has made two cups of tea.

LOUISA   It's amazing – Effie – that you're doing – so well – and your Mum – it's great

EFFIE   Yep

A beat.

LOUISA   I should take this to your Mum

LOUISA leaves the kitchen carrying a cup of tea.

EFFIE is just leaning on the unit.

She puts her face into her hands.

She lets out a horrible groan.

After a time she straightens.

She goes to the fridge and fills a glass at the water filter.

She drinks the whole glass full and the fills it again.

She goes to SALLY's bag. Takes out a bottle of pills. She swallows two pills with water.

CASTRO enters. He stops when he sees EFFIE. He goes over to the fridge and takes out a bottle of beer.

He opens the beer and starts drinking it with his back to EFFIE.

EFFIE   You looked in on her?

CASTRO   Yeah

EFFIE   She ok?

CASTRO   Yeah

A beat.

EFFIE shakes her head.

CAS drains the bottle.

He opens the fridge takes out another beer. Opens it.

EFFIE   You're getting a fat gut

Still with his back to her – he drinks.

            And then what exactly will you have to offer
            me?

She leaves.

He turns to look after her.

He rubs his stomach.

He drinks.

LOUISA enters.

CASTRO   Thank God

LOUISA   What?

CASTRO   That I get to see you

LOUISA   Castro

CASTRO   What?

LOUISA   Don't you feel

CASTRO   What?

LOUISA   A bit – sleazy – actually

A pause.

CASTRO   No

LOUISA   Well, I'm sorry but – it – and inappropriate?

CASTRO   I don't think it's my fault that every time I see
            you there is some disaster I just / like you

LOUISA   It's not about disasters or what is going on
            around you it's about the fact you're you and
            you've got a family and you say you like me you
            don't know me – so

CASTRO   I've always had a great feeling / about you

LOUISA	So stop please just stop
CASTRO	OK
LOUISA	OK
CASTRO	OK
LOUISA	Thank you

A beat.

CASTRO	No – I don't want to
LOUISA	Well tough!
CASTRO	Talk to me
LOUISA	No – about what?
CASTRO	What have you been – you know – how are you?
LOUISA	I'm doing OK thank you. It's – well you know how it's been – but –

I am happy now – or much happier than I thought it would be possible to – when Michael went to prison – well – a downturn in fortunes doesn't really tell – nothing was how it seemed – and – I lost – a – a lot – but – it was *shit* – *really* shit – but – I mean – I'm in a pretty good place. Is what I mean

CASTRO	Good. I'm glad to hear it
LOUISA	Thank you
CASTRO	You look great – you always look great
LOUISA	Thank you

A beat.

And you – this must all have been – you must be picking up a lot of pieces – for the girls – I mean

CASTRO	Not really

LOUISA   Oh, right

CASTRO   All the girls in this family can pretty much look
           after themselves

LOUISA   Yes – maybe – well that's good – but there's a
           difference between carrying on – getting on with
           things and – being OK – really OK

CASTRO   I don't really want to talk about them

LOUISA   What do you want to talk about Castro? You?

A beat.

           Sorry. That was very rude. Sorry – I'd actually
           be interested to know how things are / going on
           with you. Sorry

CASTRO   No that's alright – I'm sorry if you've ever, yeah,
           had that impression that I just want to / talk
           about me

LOUISA   No no – it's not that – I don't know you – I'm
           self conscious – so – I – maybe I'm pissed off
           with myself because *I do* want to know what
           you're up to – and that that's indiscreet – even
           – look talk – shut me up please – what are you
           doing how's the film-making going? Please

A beat.

CASTRO   Well interestingly. If you wanna get a film made,
           you have to talk about it. And talk about it. And
           talk about yourself – so – you know – sorry

LOUISA   Get on / with it

CASTRO   You have to talk and talk to money people to
           producers – to film councils – to friends – make
           sure it doesn't fade away. But talk is only talk –
           and people get sick of hearing it – and the ideas
           just start to feel like words in your own mouth
           – and you can feel real tragedies, devastating
           crimes turning into clichés – Africa blah blah
           – evil dictators blah blah – oil blah blah –

warming blah blah – extinction blah – because the world moves so fast it can't remain interested even in the most critical things – because tomorrow somewhere will flood or get blown up someone wins some competition on the TV or some prick hurts his foot kicking a ball around or some spoilt prima donna wears a fur coat and no knickers

LOUISA   Or gets her roots darkened

A beat.

CASTRO   Exactly. / Precisely

LOUISA   I can't believe I said that I'm so sorry I'm such / a bitch I'm so sorry

CASTRO   Look – don't worry. Trust me – you – I know what / she's like

LOUISA   She was just going on a bit in here before – I let it get to / me and I'm sorry

CASTRO   Look are you going to let me tell you all about me or what?

LOUISA smiles.

LOUISA   Yes – go on I'll give you five minutes! You were making a film about oil weren't you?

CASTRO   Well – it's

LOUISA   Are you still making – is that done?

CASTRO   Well – it's – there's more to it – yes I'm *making* it – but with anything like this – look – ask me something else – that's – too / big a

LOUISA   I'm interested in that – so – go on

CASTRO   You are beautiful

LOUISA   Five minutes! Go!

CASTRO laughs.

CASTRO   OK – strap yourself in.

I started off in Nigeria – the Niger Delta – Shell
– because – it's Africa and because it's Shell,
yeah? I'm sure you read about all that shit

LOUISA   Yeah yeah – a little but I'm embarrassed to say I
just don't take it in

CASTRO   Of course you don't most people don't or can't
or won't or refuse to

LOUISA   Well I read half an article then put it down

CASTRO   Because it's terrifying

LOUISA   But then – I talk about it as if I've read the whole
article – I mean – because I think I know it

CASTRO   Yes

LOUISA   I'm embarrassed to say that – so tell me – tell
me

CASTRO   In a nutshell!

He laughs.

Fifty years of drilling and pipes running through
their lands – one of the biggest wetland areas
in the world – billions and billions of dollars
poured into Nigeria – so many people making
fortunes – and the tribespeople that live in the
Delta are as poor as ever – it's made no positive
difference to their way of life – constant spillages
sending oil leaching into the ground and the
water – killing everything around – young palm
trees just falling in on themselves – black and
rotting inside out.

The big problem – the *big crime* – Gas Flares
burning and choking the environment – Gas
Flares are like big bunsons, yeah, burning
outside the oil plants – drilling fucking creates
all this extra unwanted gas and so they just burn
it off with these massive flares – gas, that if they
built the right conversion plants, could provide
for the energy needs of most of the country, is

wasted – millions of dollars literally going up in smoke.

Gas flaring – it's practically banned in the west – those flares are the largest cause of CO_2 emissions south of the Sahara.

The Delta – beautiful –

He reaches out to touch LOUISA's face and she moves away. She moves in front of some kitchen drawers.

a complex system of waterways, luscious green mangrove creeks – but it's humid, yeah. Fucking humid. So – these black clouds sit and stay above all this beauty – and all around are these noxious fumes – it stinks – and these flares – these fucking – these flares can be *seen from space*.

And the people there, they know it affects their health – we met a man – Chinna – they fed us and I was nervous – eating their food – where it has grown where it was washed – his wife, Dammi, took us to a nearby creek and put a bowl into the water – she scooped it out and it looked fine – but as it settled there was a thin darkish oily film on the top, yeah, and a kind of black dust on the bottom – this is where they wash – they now have to try and buy bottled water to drink and to cook with – Dammi put her hand in the bowl and held it up in front of the camera

CASTRO illustrates with his own hand.

and said, 'We are living with death!'

LOUISA   Jesus. It's horrible / devastating

CASTRO   Who knows about this?

Who cares?

The local community fucking cares and that community has been at war with these oil companies about this kind of shit for, like, over thirty years.

He goes to a wine rack and checks out a couple of reds while he talks.

There is consistent damage to the pipelines so oil is constantly leaking in to the waterways, yeah?

Rebel leaders who wanted to know why their people are living in poverty and with their lives at risk when 80 per cent of the country's revenue comes from the oil fields that are destroying their homelands and communities – some of these rebels have been fucking executed. The government and the oil companies won. Call the rebels terrorists and thieves – blame them for the pipeline damage and the leaks – and kill them. And now the people can't even trust their rebels – armed gangs living outside the law – dressed like fucking hip hop gangsters and moving around the waterways armed to the fucking teeth with AK47s – claiming to be fighting for the communities but half the time just acting like Highwaymen – taking big pay-offs from the government and from the oil companies, who are sick of the raids on the oil pipes, to slow down their activities – stop attacking oil drilling plants – stop kidnapping foreign oil company workers. So these 'rebels' end up sitting around smoking weed and playing with their AKs – it's a fucking mess. And the people that suffer? The people who aren't getting any handouts? The poor people who live there!

But

luckily

there has been a *report*

He has made his way over to LOUISA. They are quite close.

LOUISA   Castro!

CASTRO   I need to get in there

He points to a drawer behind her. She moves to the other side of the kitchen.

LOUISA   The report.

He removes a corkscrew form the drawer and opens the wine as he talks.

CASTRO   There was a detailed environmental report and it only blamed Shell for ten per cent of the leaks and bursts over the years – saying the naughty rebels and terrorists were responsible. Only ten per cent of the blame lay with Shell. But who commissioned the report? Shell!

LOUISA   No!

CASTRO   I

            I mean – can't we see – what's going on – can't we see it – why aren't we asking fucking questions about this?

LOUISA   So is this your documentary? This should be your film

CASTRO   It was it was – and then someone – I mean it could be

LOUISA   Yes yes – you have to / make this

CASTRO   Of course it *could* be – but then I started to read about Sakhalin Island. East Russia – in the North Pacific. Sakhalin is a difficult place to get to. Seven fucking time zones from Moscow – Shell got in there and the Japanese oil companies, Mitsubishi and Mitsui I think it is – anyway – it's so inhospitable – that they can pretty much go on undetected – it's way way North – off the coast – icy – the Mamiya Strait that separates it from the mainland freezes in the winter.

He takes two wine glasses from a cupboard.

So – it's, like, pretty isolated – unheard of pretty much. Crucially, yeah, it's so difficult for any kind of environmental organisation to get near it – and if you do get there, yeah, two thirds of it is mountainous and in the winter temperatures can get down to minus 45 degrees. *Basically* it's fucking freezing and fucking miles away.

He pours two glasses of wine.

At first the Russians were, like, all over it, yeah? All over Shell and the Japanese – for all the right reasons – saying that the oil companies had not matched up to – or hadn't complied or something – with the Environmental Drilling Assessment. So – it all goes quiet for a while – then – suddenly – *Gazprom* – the Russian oil gas energy giant are *a partner* and now the Russians are all over it for a whole host of other reasons and the environmental welfare stuff isn't mentioned anymore. Convenient.

He takes a glass over to LOUISA.

It's a disaster for the environment

LOUISA   I don't really

CASTRO   Drink with me please.

Please.

LOUISA takes the glass.

There are about one hundred and thirty Western Grey Wales left – on the planet – and only about 30 reproductive females – and where is their feeding ground – off the shore of Sakhalin island – all the fucking seismic activity of these drilling platforms, yeah, is affecting the sonar communication of the whales – they are all over the shop – they can't find each other – they can't calculate their distance from the shore – the whales have been beaching – and do you know about this? Who knows? Who fucking cares?

The Russians have managed to stop all images of the beached whales from circulating. Unfuckingbelievable.

The whole marine environment is gonna be fucked – thousands of fishermen – fucked.

Indigenous people – who live off the sea who lived off the land – who when these fuckers turned up were still riding reindeers bareback.

The energy companies move in and – oh yeah, that's another thing, yeah – you know you think about the oil companies and you think of Texans in suits and cowboy boots in big boardrooms or you think of the construction workers, in checked shirts chewin' tobacco, who put the drilling and pipelining into operation, yeah? But it's *engineers* – it's *geologists* – *scientists*! What the fuck are these dudes playing at? Money money money – putting their kids through school, whatever!

Company men – 'he's a company man' – bullied and scared – these company men – keep your head down keep your mouth shut honour the company name and reap the fucking benefits.

And their presence, their money and the fact this place is so difficult to get to so hard to import luxuries into has made Sakhalin the most expensive place on the planet – so how are the indigenous people expected to survive and the Russian and Vietnamese communities that have been there for half a century?

LOUISA   I don't know I can't keep / up it's too much

CASTRO   Crime and prostitution has gone through the roof.

And this massive influx of mostly male – foreign workers hasn't just generated this – harrowing – fucking rise in prostitution, but also violence against the women and fucking HIV – it's a – that island is like a nightmare.

But it's so important, Sakhalin is so important, because it points in the direction that the energy giants are going to go.

The oil is getting harder and harder to find – previously unreachable territories up in the Arctic – and although this is a *challenge* to the energy companies it's also a fucking *advantage* – because we can't get out there to see what they're doing.

Look the pattern is – it's like a sick joke – the carbons we burn heat up the planet – it melts the ice – these fuckers follow the melting ice and it's easier to drill in more and more obscure, difficult as fuck to get to, parts of the planet.

Unwatched.

They are waiting – the British the Americans the Norwegians the Danes the Canadians the Russians to just carve up the Arctic.

As the ice melts you've got shipping routes, yeah, that previously were only navigable in the summer months, that are open all year now making it much easier for them to get in there, yeah – get equipment in there – and start drilling.

There's gonna be an Oil Rush in these – vulnerable – unspoilt waters and lands.

They're getting further and further away from us – and we are getting further and further away from the truth.

And there are only two voices to listen to here, yeah – the environmental agencies who say this is going to be a disaster and the energy companies who say it can be done with, like, minimal impact – like the minimal impact in the Niger Delta or the fucking Deepwater Disaster or Sakhalin Island. But which voice do you think the governments will listen to?

And why? Because of people like us. People who vote governments in and out of office because of fuel bills or the cost of petrol at the pump.

He gets more and more passionate during the following.

We don't want to pay more so we vote governments out.

We've stopped asking questions.

We have a lifestyle that we like and we don't want to pay more for it.

As long as we keep sending governments this message they're going to keep drilling and the more shit we are going to get ourselves in.

Coz the real damage the real crimes are taking place as they fight to get hold of the last of the oil.

We need to stop thinking about ourselves and what we can give our kids – stop thinking about ourselves – stop thinking about our spoilt children and think about our children's children.

And this stuff is going to run out. When we've finished there will be no oil – no natural gas – left. A fucked up planet with no fuel. Genius.

You bored to death yet? My five minutes / must be up

LOUISA   No – no of course not but what do / we do?

CASTRO   It's our fault – as long as we keep talking about an energy crisis and not an environmental crisis.

And people don't want to hear it – because it is boring – people don't want to hear people

talking about it – they don't wanna hear me
bang on about the films I'm making – wanna
make – and the content – People Are Dying –
yes we know but not while we're eating please
– People Are Being Fucking Ripped Off In The
Name Of Big Fat Corporate Profit – come on
man we're on a night out have a drink relax –
The World Is Dying The Energy Companies Are
Killing Us – I know, we know, but come on look
at the kids, when you watch them playing and
laughing how can you worry about anything else
– not now – please not now it's boring boring
boring talk talk talk – no one wants to hear it

LOUISA   But, people, do they just need it to really be
            brought to their attention?

CASTRO   There is one environmental report after another

LOUISA   Yes – maybe – but

CASTRO   But there is no real will – to change

He drains his wine glass.

LOUISA   But people give – to charity – err – Aid –
            disaster funds – I did charity work alongside
            Michael – silly stuff celebrity stuff – well no –
            not silly – it meant – something – of course – to
            the beneficiaries – but I loved it – because –
            even when he went to prison – our divorce – the
            money I got – I made two big – sizable – final
            – gestures – because – then you are *doing* stuff –
            but I had all the charity work taken away from
            me

CASTRO is refilling his glass.

CASTRO   People aren't asking the big questions

LOUISA   You are – I want to – they said I was tainted –
            my name – by what Michael did

CASTRO   Charity is just disposable cash

LOUISA   It wasn't disposable – it was all – pretty / much –
            all I had

CASTRO   Charity is not about changing your own fucking
            life. We've stopped asking questions. We don't
            want to change because there is too much of
            what we've learnt to love to lose and too much
            money to be lost if those changes are made

LOUISA   Listen / I want to help you

She goes to him.

CASTRO   People aren't doing anything

LOUISA   You are – I think I would – *you are*

She puts her hand on his chest. Holding his shirt front in her fist.

CASTRO   No I'm not – I'm just talking to you about it –
            I'm stood in a very nice kitchen at a very nice
            drinks party talking to you about it

EFFIE enters.

EFFIE   It's not a drinks party – it's my Dad's funeral

A pause.

CASTRO   Oh yeah

EFFIE   Are you looking for another investor?

CASTRO   Go away, Effie

EFFIE   Louisa – are you looking to invest – in my
            husband?

LOUISA   I have nothing to invest, Effie

EFFIE   He used to be very talented you know

A pause.

            We've managed to get rid of everyone

A pause.

            Well. Not *everyone*.

SALLY enters

SALLY   That's it. All gone. Are you OK, Louisa?

LOUISA   Yes thank you

SALLY   Well now it's really too late to try and get back
          to the sticks. So you're staying

LOUISA   Yes. I'd like to

SALLY   Oh, fantastic – lovely

The doorbell rings.

          Oh

EFFIE   It'll be that Australian woman

CASTRO   I'll go

He heads out of the kitchen.

EFFIE   She'll have forgotten something – like the last
          dregs of her personality

SALLY   Oh God – she really is pretty awful

LOUISA   Who did you say she was?

SALLY   Daniel's new lady

EFFIE   Lady?

SALLY   He – Daniel – he was our neighbour – his wife
          died of MS – and he used to sit out the back –
          when we had the place in Blackheath – and have
          a beer with Gordon

EFFIE   Or ten beers with Gordon

SALLY   Yes. It gets hold of so many men doesn't it?

EFFIE   Looks like

SALLY   I didn't fight it

EFFIE   Why should we?

SALLY   For you – maybe I should have – for you –
             fought more – but I just didn't want to think
             about it. *Dirty* Beer my dad used to call it. Dirty

*She stops short as CASTRO walks in with MICHAEL. MICHAEL looks
older. Drawn. He is wearing cheap jeans and cheap trainers.*

             Michael?

MICHAEL   Hello, Sally.

             Hello, Sal.

*Instinctively SALLY goes over to MICHAEL and embraces him. They hold
each other.*

             Don't, Love. You'll have me crying my heart out

She holds his face in his hands.

SALLY   Hello, Michael

MICHAEL   Hello.

             Louisa

LOUISA   Hello

MICHAEL   I thought you would have gone, Louisa, I'm
             sorry. I've been watching people leave. I just
             thought – sorry

SALLY   Have you been sat outside?

MICHAEL   I've been stood outside

SALLY   Michael

MICHAEL   I needed to see you

SALLY   You didn't need to – but thank you – thank you,
             Michael

MICHAEL   *(To LOUISA.)* I wanted to pay my respects

LOUISA   Of course

MICHAEL   You understand that?

LOUISA   Yes

SALLY   Of course, Darling

MICHAEL   Hello, Effie

EFFIE   Hi

MICHAEL   I'm really very sorry about your Dad

EFFIE   Thanks

SALLY   Do you want a drink? Food? Do you want
                something to eat?

A beat.

MICHAEL   I...

SALLY   What?

MICHAEL   I'd love something – if that's OK?

SALLY   Of course of course there's so much food left –
                Cas – will you get Michael a drink?

SALLY starts putting a plate of food together from various trays.

CASTRO   What can I get you?

MICHAEL   A whisky – would be good – warm me up

CASTRO   Ice?

MICHAEL   What's the whisky?

CASTRO   Dunno – it's in

He indicates towards the living room.

MICHAEL   Err – no – no ice

CASTRO heads off.

                And thank you, Castro

SALLY   Sausage rolls, Michael

MICHAEL   Lovely – proper food

SALLY   Big ones

MICHAEL   Great

SALLY   With sage and apricot

MICHAEL   Fancy

SALLY   Yes – they're a bit too rich though – very rich –
and some risotto – and – oh, do you want any of
this heated up?

MICHAEL   No – God no – that's fine

SALLY   Some salads

SALLY keeps plating up as the others watch.

Silence.

CASTRO enters and hands the glass to MICHAEL.

CASTRO   Jamesons

MICHAEL   Oh – OK – fine – thank you

CASTRO picks up his wine glass and drains it. He goes to the fridge and takes out a beer for himself. And opens it.

SALLY   Here you go, Michael

She hands over the food.

MICHAEL   Thank you

He stands holding the plate in one hand the glass in the other.

SALLY   Sit down.

She indicates the stools at the breakfast bar.

MICHAEL stands there.

Michael

MICHAEL   I need to speak to you, Sally. And maybe Effie.
And maybe Castro

SALLY   OK

A beat.

LOUISA   I'll go next door

MICHAEL   Sorry

LOUISA   No no that's fine

| SALLY | OK Louisa? |
| LOUISA | Yes – of course – fine |

LOUISA goes out. MICHAEL puts his plate and glass down. He picks up the sausage roll and takes a big bite.

MICHAEL	I'm really sorry about Gordon
SALLY	Thank you
MICHAEL	He was the best friend I ever had

He takes another big bite.

He abandoned me

He looks at them.

He abandoned me

EFFIE	He was disgusted at what you did
MICHAEL	Everybody was disgusted at what I did – I heard that everywhere –
	I read that everywhere
EFFIE	How many counts of sexual
MICHAEL	Everyone was disgusted. When I / was charged
EFFIE	Assault
MICHAEL	When I was prosecuted – during / my time in prison
EFFIE	Harrassment
MICHAEL	Everyone was disgusted
EFFIE	Yes
MICHAEL	Not everyone was my best friend
EFFIE	Fuck you

MICHAEL takes another bite.

I said fuck you

| SALLY | Effie, please |

EFFIE   No – fuck off – coming in here – *today* – it was his funeral today you fucking idiot – coming in here eating our food – drinking Dad's whisky and – what the fuck? Like – like – like who / the fuck do you think you are?

SALLY   Effie calm down – please, Baby /don't

EFFIE   Some, like, some fucking old perv coming in here and slagging him off and telling us, like, what? That he, like, let you down?

MICHAEL   Yes I am saying that – yes / I am

EFFIE   What the fuck?

MICHAEL   I'm your Godfather, Effie

EFFIE   What? Like – So?

MICHAEL   Your Dad thought that counted / for a lot

EFFIE   So? So? You dick. Fuckoff

SALLY   Effie I'm not going to tell you again stop it

EFFIE   I'm not taking any shit from him

SALLY   Be quiet, Effie. I mean it – please – be quiet

EFFIE stops. She is steaming.

MICHAEL   I'm sorry, Sally

SALLY   Michael

MICHAEL   I've been talking to Gordon – for months – trying to get him to be fair about everything

A beat.

SALLY   Fair about what?

MICHAEL   Oh, come on

SALLY   What do you mean?

MICHAEL   Come on, Love

SALLY   What?

What?

MICHAEL   I need to be paid back – it's – look at me now –
                 my circumstances

A beat.

SALLY   I don't get – I don't understand / what you're
                 getting at

MICHAEL   Tax man – three civil lawsuits – Louisa –
                 compensation – everything was mortgaged – re-
                 mortgaged – and / damages

EFFIE   What do you mean – *paid back?*

MICHAEL   He cut me off – OK – everybody did – OK.
                 He – abandoned me – and – I tried to get hold
                 of him from inside – he had a different mobile
                 number from when I knew – from before. This
                 place – I didn't have an address for this place – I
                 didn't even know you'd moved – it's very nice
                 by the way

SALLY   Thank you

MICHAEL   And when I got hold of him – nothing – I could
                 have come around here before – but I didn't –
                 out of respect to you – for you – I didn't – so
                 – I only knew yesterday that he had died – no
                 one thought to tell me – I heard from my sister
                 that Clare had contacted her and said she was
                 coming to England to Gordon's funeral – you
                 told Clare you didn't tell me

SALLY   I didn't know where you were

MICHAEL   Gordon did

SALLY   I didn't know that

MICHAEL   I want that money – I need that – you can't –
                 you have to see – you've got to make sure I get
                 paid back.

A beat.

	I fuckin' – I'm going to get it back
SALLY	Money?
MICHAEL	Money
SALLY	What money?
MICHAEL	Sally
EFFIE	What fucking money?
SALLY	Effie!
MICHAEL	Two hundred and fifty thousand pounds

A beat.

SALLY	I don't / understand
EFFIE	What?
MICHAEL	That's what I'm owed
EFFIE	What do you mean?
MICHAEL	Sally
SALLY	What?
MICHAEL	Come on, Sally, please – don't pretend – don't treat me like a piece of dirt – please, Sally, please
SALLY	Are you saying Gordon owed you that?
MICHAEL	Sally
SALLY	What? Are you?
MICHAEL	You know – don't pretend – you all – *(To EFFIE.)* you knew that day – you all came around – one big happy family – Sally please
EFFIE	We don't know what you're fucking talking about
SALLY	We don't, Michael – truly – yes – I mean – we came around to your house – when Effie was pregnant
EFFIE	Two hundred and fifty thousand pounds?

SALLY   But, Michael – Gordon asked you for ten – you
               gave him ten thousand pounds – to pay off his
               overdraft and – we were behind with a few
               mortgage payments

EFFIE   You liar

SALLY   He – I mean – we still lost that flat – he lost all
               his money – I'm my own business – I made sure
               I kept it separate as Gordon was – with money –
               you know

EFFIE   He was fucking useless

SALLY   Any money I have is mine – his business

MICHAEL   I was an investor in that business – I had –
               money in there – of the two hundred and
               fifty thousand pounds, one hundred and fifty
               thousand of it went into that business

EFFIE   What? You put, like, over a hundred grand
               into a gardening business? One man and a
               borrowed lawn mower?

MICHAEL   He told me he was going to expand – that it
               was – landscaping – whatever – that he – that
               we – were doing it for you and your daughter –
               building a future for you

EFFIE   You and him? Don't make me fucking laugh

MICHAEL   That he had dreams – that you thought he was
               pathetic that you compared him to me – that
               he wanted his respect back – I gave him two
               hundred and fifty thousand pounds and I want it
               back – from you or from you

SALLY   He told me that you were a partner – but that
               you weren't a – a what is i, Effie – when you
               have money / in a

MICHAEL   Shareholder

SALLY   Yes

EFFIE   There were no shareholders – don't make me
               laugh

MICHAEL   I was

SALLY   No – I mean Gordon said it was just about using
            your name – that

EFFIE   Your name – what a joke – your / good name

SALLY   He was insolvent – he told me – I mean I knew
            you couldn't be a director – that – *he* knew that
            – *I* knew that – that when you went to prison –
            that that disqualified you from being a / director

MICHAEL   But that wouldn't affect my investment. I have
            the papers we drew up

EFFIE   I'm the executor – my lawyer is – there was
            never any money paid into that business in your
            name or anyone else's

MICHAEL   I gave him cash

EFFIE   You gave him one hundred and fifty thousand
            pounds in cash?

MICHAEL   Two hundred and fifty thousand pounds in cash

EFFIE   What in, like, in, like, a suitcase?

MICHAEL   He said it was for you – so you'd respect him
            again – that you wanted him to be like me – that
            it was for Effie – for his beautiful daughter – my
            god-daughter – he kept saying that she's your
            god-daughter – that it was – what did that mean
            – he convinced me that it meant something – for
            his child and her child, his – what is she called
            – his Granddaughter – about fucking family –
            about fucking love

SALLY   Farai

MICHAEL   Yes – fucking Farai and Effie

EFFIE   Don't! Don't say fucking and / her name

MICHAEL   That's mine that money it's not yours or hers it's
            mine

SALLY   Michael you have to listen to me we didn't know – I don't know anything about this money

MICHAEL   I was always so good to you to all of you

SALLY   Yes yes

MICHAEL   And do I deserve this?

SALLY   Michael – this is not about us or / about Gordon

MICHAEL   It is of course it is

SALLY   You went to prison – you lost everything – you did that not us – you did that –

MICHAEL   That doesn't make any difference – you owe me that money – you've got it

SALLY   I don't have two hundred and – I – I don't have access to that kind of money

EFFIE   Castro

CASTRO   What?

EFFIE   Say something

CASTRO   Effie

EFFIE   What? Fucking what? You are so wet. You are – be a man please, Castro

CASTRO   Leave it

EFFIE   Leave what?

CASTRO   Don't start with me

EFFIE   How can you? Like? How? What he is saying about me about Farai / about your daughter

CASTRO   He isn't saying anything about Farai

EFFIE   So it's OK for him to talk to Mum and me like this

CASTRO   I don't think it's any of my business

MICHAEL   Sell this house

SALLY   Michael – this is for my family

MICHAEL   Your family – your fucking family is what got me in this shit – I've always been good to you always always

SALLY   Not always

MICHAEL   Always

SALLY   Gordon treated me badly – he was – you treated people badly and the two of you – covered – and

MICHAEL   I loved you, Sally I've always loved you you were my / real friend – always

SALLY   I remember things

EFFIE   You are useless you don't say anything you can't do anything what are you you're a waste of space you pseudo fucking useless heartless twat. I'll do it – I'll get rid of him

EFFIE pulls a knife off a magnetic strip on the wall.

CASTRO   Don't be a dick, Effie. Fuckin' put that down

EFFIE   GET OUT

LOUISA has come back into the kitchen.

MICHAEL   Gordon told me you thought that I was the one – I mean I could have been the one – that maybe you / and me

SALLY   YOU FUCKING LAUGHED AT ME YOU ALWAYS DID ALL THREE OF YOU YOU

LAUGHED AT ME I WAS THE RUNT OF
THE LITTER THE LAP DOG YOUR 'IN
JOKE' YOU AND HIM THE BASTARD
AND THAT BITCH

Everyone is looking at SALLY now. Shocked at the ferociousness of the outburst.

EFFIE   Mum?

SALLY   Even on my wedding night I couldn't trust
            the three of you – Gordon and her – tell me,
            Michael – what did they do? What happened?
            Your best friend – my best friend. She's been
            floating around here today – and she knows
            something – Clare – it makes me vomit – Clare
            – she's got something on me and it makes me –
            living with that. Having to live with that – from
            that first morning smelling all your sweat and
            three greedy dirty pigs all folded up together in
            my bed – in my honeymoon suite – living with
            that. Your wife – my husband – she was here
            again in my life and knowing something that I
            don't know and you know how much that gives
            her and takes away from me – power – God it
            was good to see her and feel *hate* – just to feel
            it – all of you did that to me – my husband, your
            wife and you I guess – and you. I never thought
            you were capable – but now I know what you're
            capable of.

            (To LOUISA.) I'm sorry, Louisa.

            (To MICHAEL.) What happened?

A long pause.

MICHAEL   I want my money, Sally

LOUISA   Just go Michael – leave us alone

SALLY   I know anyway – I know – I've always

EFFIE   What?

MICHAEL	Louisa – help me – you know about the money I gave to Gordon
SALLY	Him – your father and Clare
LOUISA	You were stupid – I told you you were stupid
EFFIE	What about them?
MICHAEL	I was trying to help – see – see – she knows – Louisa tell them
SALLY	Sex – OK – fucking each other all /of them on my wedding night
LOUISA	Everything you ever did was stupid – greedy – a / waste – and it affects everybody
EFFIE	I'm going to be sick
MICHAEL	I want what's mine
LOUISA	Selfish
MICHAEL	It is *mine*
LOUISA	And what about what's mine – that you – what you took from me – I had a – some sort of – life
MICHAEL	What – giving all my money away?
LOUISA	I got to do things that I thought were making a little difference
MICHAEL	*MINE!*

EFFIE runs at MICHAEL – she hits and pulls at him – he covers his head and lets her.

EFFIE   The way you've always made me feel you've always *looked* at me I knew even when I was little

CASTRO half attempts to pull her away.

FUCKOFF CASTRO

you looked – in my swimming costumes – everything – always there when Mum – and my Mum you've hurt my Mum you bastard –when I needed to change – you did didn't you

you looked – the stuff I wore for dancing for
swimming – watching – DIDN'T YOU?

MICHAEL stands suddenly – strong – throws her away.

MICHAEL YES I FUCKING DID YES I DID YES I
DID WHO CARES WHO CARES ABOUT
YOU YOU SPOILT LITTLE WHORE WHO
FUCKING CARES?

Pause. People trying to recover from this explosion.

 HEYY?

Still no one speaks.

 AAAAAAGGGGGGGHHHHHHHH!

A pause.

LOUISA Just go

EFFIE Yes go – please – just fucking go

MICHAEL It was always about you – always about
everyone else – about what you haven't got –
what you wanted – how I could help – but now
you can help me

EFFIE We don't want to

MICHAEL Louisa – just tell them that please – nothing
else just tell them – I *need* – just tell them that
you know – you fucking know what I gave to
Gordon

 Louisa?

 Fucking

 I was helping I was trying – Louisa?

 Please

 Tell them

 Please

LOUISA You took everything from me that I liked – I was
helping people, Michael

MICHAEL   Help me – help me – I haven't got anything

EFFIE   Tough shit

MICHAEL   No home – no money – no friends – no help –
no work – no children – no hope – nothing to
look forward to

EFFIE   Good – tough fucking shit

MICHAEL   I'd love to smash you – you've always – you
spiteful hateful little

EFFIE   Fucking what? Like, Hello

LOUISA   Effie – pick up the phone and call the police and
tell them that Michael Stewart is in your home
against your wishes and won't leave

They all think about this.

LOUISA   Do it, Effie

EFFIE goes to the phone.

Michael – I don't know the conditions of your
release – but I'm damn sure that a young
woman – in distress – ringing the police is not
going to do you any favours. Go

EFFIE has dialled.

CASTRO   You should just go

MICHAEL   FUCK

EFFIE   Hello – yes – Michael fucking Stewart is in my
fucking house he's fucking sick

LOUISA   Go, Michael

MICHAEL   There is a way I will get this I will

EFFIE   Effie – Effie Blechman

MICHAEL   Sally – I'm on my knees – Gordon said – he said
it was about friendship, Sally – I'm begging you
– trust, Sally – family, Sally

EFFIE   73 Denmark Hill

SALLY	I didn't trust any of you. And I had to try and get through every day without that. Without trust.
EFFIE	Camberwell
LOUISA	Michael
EFFIE	He's in my Mother's house – yes – Michael Stewart
MICHAEL	Louisa
LOUISA	Go

MICHAEL goes.

EFFIE waits. Holding phone away from her. They hear the door slam. She puts the phone down.

CASTRO	*(To LOUISA.)* You were amazing
LOUISA	Make sure he's gone

CASTRO goes out.

The telephone rings.

SALLY	Who is that?
LOUISA	It'll be the police.

LOUISA goes to the phone. Picks up.

> Hello.
>
> Yes – we did.
>
> No everything's fine – we panicked unnecessarily.
>
> What's the address here?

SALLY	73 Denmark Hill, Camberwell
LOUISA	73 Denmark Hill, Camberwell

CASTRO enters.

CASTRO	I'm pretty sure he's gone.

LOUISA   We thought someone was trying to get in – but it was a mistaken identity – it was someone we knew – a friend,

Yes.

No.

All good here – honestly. Sorry to have wasted your time.

OK then.

Thank you very much.

Bye

She puts the phone down.

SALLY   You're amazing

LOUISA   Don't be silly

CASTRO   You are

LOUISA   I know Michael

A beat

Well

SALLY   I feel sorry for him – but

A beat.

I think I'm going to be sick

She moves to the door.

EFFIE   Oh, God – I'll come with you.

She starts to follow – rushes back and takes pills back from SALLY's bag.

Her pills.

She gets to the door. She turns back and looks at LOUISA and CASTRO.

What was it, Castro?

CASTRO   What was what?

She holds up her hand with an open palm.

'We are living with death'

EFFIE   What? No – like – truth – something – openness

CASTRO   Oh – yeah

EFFIE   Transparency

She puts hers hand down and leaves.

LOUISA   What does she mean?

CASTRO   Nothing

LOUISA   It didn't look like nothing

CASTRO   Just – another film – another – that I haven't
            made – have been making – for years – trying to
            make – about Zimbabwe

LOUISA   Where your mother is from?

CASTRO   She's from Zambia – but

LOUISA   Why don't you do something? Finish something

CASTRO   Why don't you help me?

LOUISA   How? I'm worse than you. I've never done
            anything. Charity – disposable income

CASTRO   The most difficult thing is moving the material
            around – the film – the tapes – discs – they
            search anything that looks like it might be
            related to the media – and of course we have
            to get cameras in and out – however small – so
            we usually have to rely on people – sometimes
            just sympathetic westerners who we've met
            in bars – or hotel lobbies – to get stuff out for
            us – sometimes friends have flown in – people
            who look respectable don't look like scruffs who
            work in the media – don't look like a part of a
            guerrilla documentary film crew – people like
            you actually – smart – conservative-looking

LOUISA   Is that what you think of me?

CASTRO   You don't want to know what I think of you

A beat.

LOUISA   Yes I do

CASTRO   I think you're beautiful – I fantasise about you

A pause.

So?

LOUISA   Is this how you get smart conservative-looking
            women to do all your dirty work for you?

CASTRO   No – I don't want you to do anything for me – I
            want you to go to bed with me

A pause.

LOUISA   And then what?

CASTRO   I think – I feel like – I want to run away

LOUISA   Castro – if you 'ran off' with me. You'd have
            to stop talking about all the things you believe
            in. And do something. You'd have to work.
            I couldn't – I wouldn't – I couldn't keep you.
            You're on a fucking good thing here. And you
            know it

CASTRO   I don't want to be here anymore

LOUISA   What about Farai?

CASTRO   I'm not convinced that this is the best – kind – of
            – family – in fact – family – Jesus – it's a fucking
            joke – we're just bouncing around – hating each
            other

He goes over to her.

Please.

He kisses her.

After some time she pushes him away.

Please

SALLY walks in.

SALLY	Oh God, are you two OK?
CASTRO	Yes. Yes. Are you OK, Louisa?
LOUISA	I think so
SALLY	That must have been worse for you than / any of us
LOUISA	It's just the shock
SALLY	Of course, Darling. It is shocking. The way people end up. Friends. It's so shocking. Are you OK, Cas?
CASTRO	Yeah fine. We should just forget all that
SALLY	Yes.

A beat. The lights start to fade on the scene.

It is shocking though. What people say and do to each other. To get what they want. Isn't it?

As the light has nearly gone. EFFIE enters – into her own light.

EPILOGUE

EFFIE   Well Farai has her own blog now – all about children's fashion and music and stuff – she doesn't write it herself obviously – Castro does it – and they make little films together – cute. Little films about how to grow things, planting seeds – and, like, helping mummy and daddy with recycling – all that stuff.

And – it works for us – I'm so busy – and changing direction – if we can – I suspended production in India – and found a factory in Spain where we can – nowhere near as cheaply – but I finally got out to Mumbai – and I'd been lied to basically – I was so fucking naive. It *was* a sweatshop – maybe there are a lot worse – I'm sure there are but – the conditions were really really upsetting. There were thirty-forty women working in this dirty hot room, no windows, lots of young girls and two little things who were probably only a couple of years older than Farai. You know, like, fuck that.

And Castro has helped me figure out how I can sponsor those two little girls and put them through school.

My board told me maybe I wasn't cut out for business.

But we're doing OK and the Mummy and Daughter clothes range has been re-introduced.

And Castro takes more of an interest.

Since he got back

He disappeared or left or ran away or fucked off for no more than 6 months.

Well it didn't take long.

For him to realise. For him to, like, get it.

He came home and I could see it. A change. He looked guilty – like a murderer.

So – we didn't even speak about it. Not really. I knew where he'd been. I know what he *said* he was doing. And I know, like, what he *was* doing and who he was with.

Mum – didn't – she didn't hear from her directly – and for Mum it's just another betrayal – someone close who let her down – but she's *heard* that Louisa is still in Africa. Working with some sort of NGO – I dunno. She'll die there, I guess, feeling good about herself, about her *contribution.*

And Castro – he's just a Dad – he does all that – as I get busier and busier – he – like, fills all the gaps.

We'll be OK I'm sure – well not, I don't know
– we'll have to be because – and – this is so
exciting – I'm pregnant – and – like – wait for
it – it's, like, fucking twins.

Which is amazing – none of my friends have
had twins.

So – we're picking names – Cas said, he used to
sit in the pub thinking up the names of all the
films he was going to make – and now he sits
at the local pool – watching Farai learn how to
swim – thinking up the names of her brother
and sister.

We found out the sex.

For the little girl we think it'll be nice to have
another Shona name – Farai means rejoice.
Isn't that amazing? I love that. So we have a few
options – Dudzai, which means be truthful – but
Cas is – very sensitive about that thinks it's an
attack.

Which maybe it is.

But the favourite – at the moment – is Dananai
– which means love one another – which for
twins, I think, is just, like, perfect. Isn't it?

And with a little grandson on the way we've
talked a lot about my dad. I fucking – miss my
dad. *Now,* I do. Like – he was my dad. I miss
him – there I've said it. My mum has been
digging photographs out, of me when I was
Farai's age – with my dad holding me. And
you can see – how he felt. He loves me. I've
been scanning them and putting them out on
Facebook and my favourite is on the Homepage
of my website. My dad's got this long Eighties
fringe and this skin tight navy blue, Fred Perry
T-shirt on and he looks so fucking cool. And I'm
so blond and chubby and cute.

And missing him

The

Feeling can get so, like, intense

That – in naming the twins – we thought the baby boy – well we thought it would be great to give his grandson my dad's name.

But

Gordon?

Gordon

I don't think so

You just couldn't do that to a child, could you?

The End.